TEACHABLE POINTS

TEACHABLE POINTS
A Guided Tour for Frontline Supervisors

REGINALD W. SYKES SR.

Lean Six Sigma Black Belt (LSSBB)

"What you learn, you teach."

iUniverse LLC
Bloomington

Teachable Points
A Guided Tour for Frontline Supervisors

Copyright © 2010, 2013 by Reginald W. Sykes Sr.

All rights reserved. No part of this book may be used or reproduced by any means, graphic, electronic, or mechanical, including photocopying, recording, taping or by any information storage retrieval system without the written permission of the publisher except in the case of brief quotations embodied in critical articles and reviews.

iUniverse books may be ordered through booksellers or by contacting:

iUniverse LLC
1663 Liberty Drive
Bloomington, IN 47403
www.iuniverse.com
1-800-Authors (1-800-288-4677)

Because of the dynamic nature of the Internet, any web addresses or links contained in this book may have changed since publication and may no longer be valid. The views expressed in this work are solely those of the author and do not necessarily reflect the views of the publisher, and the publisher hereby disclaims any responsibility for them.

Any people depicted in stock imagery provided by Thinkstock are models, and such images are being used for illustrative purposes only.
Certain stock imagery © Thinkstock.

ISBN: 978-1-4759-9771-2 (sc)
ISBN: 978-1-4759-9772-9 (ebk)

Library of Congress Control Number: 2013915753

Printed in the United States of America

iUniverse rev. date: 10/03/2013

Reggie does an excellent job using his years of experience and training to articulate real-world solutions to everyday issues in the workplace. I highly encourage supervisors to read this book and continue reading it to ensure maximum performance in their operations and team at all times throughout their career. This is a practical book that emphasizes "experienced learning."

Chad Barrow
CEO and President
Coastal Logistics Group Inc.
Corporate Division

This book is an excellent reference tool for a frontline supervisor. It provides informative lessons that can be used to be successful in any endeavor. The value of quality service, communication, efficient business processes, and personal responsibility are keys to a stable organization. Reggie's presentation is outstanding. I highly recommend this book!

Charles Hodges
CPA

Teachable Points: A Guided Tour for Frontline Supervisors is a book I would recommend to managers, supervisors, or anyone with supervisory aspirations wanting to continually improve their performance capability. In his book, Reginald Sykes stresses the value of experience, but in the context of several key words about personal behavior: commitment, discipline, diligence, and trust.

Pete Liakakis
Chairman, Chatham County (GA) Commission
(2005–12)
Vice Chairman, Savannah (GA) City Council
(1996–2003)

Reginald Sykes has delivered a well-written manual that is both practical and easy to read. The book is reflective of the wisdom and insights that come from the mind and heart of one who has been a lifelong learner and teacher. You will greatly profit by learning and living these Teachable Points.

Kenny Grant Sr.
Pastor
Kenny Grant Evangelistic Ministries (K-GEM)

To my dear bride, JoAnne, who has always stood by my side: your courage has always strengthened me, and so I just want to say thank you for being who you are and making me what I am. For when I've needed you the most, there you've stood.

And to my five children and all of my grandchildren and great-grandchildren: my love for each of you is immeasurable. With your presence in my life, there is nothing more that I need to be joyful each and every day.

CONTENTS

Foreword xi
Preface xiii
Introduction xvii

1 General Operating Principles 1
    a) The Purpose of the Frontline Supervisor
    b) Effective Management and Use of Resources
    c) The Work Process
    d) Plan—Do—Check—Act (PDCA)
    e) Personnel
    f) Employee Satisfaction
    g) Equipment
    h) Safety
    i) Your Personal Performance—Your Personal Goals

2 Frontline Supervision: A Challenging Position 22
3 Service: The Purpose of Business 26
4 Customers and Their Expectations 28
    a) Getting and Keeping the Customer
    b) Being On Point
    c) Service Commitment
    d) Predictably Unpredictable
    e) Service and Yesterday's Value
    f) Concentric Circles

5 Your Performance: Back to Basics 49
    a) The Three Cs: Communication, Cooperation, and Commitment

    b) Learn to Dialogue
    c) Good, Better, Better, Better . . .
    d) Nine Points to Master

6 Managing Your Personnel.. 70
    a) Getting Results through People
    b) Operating from a Base of Honesty and Sincerity

Notes... 79

Foreword

Dear reader,

Teachable Points: A Guided Tour for Frontline Supervisors is an outstanding tool for both new managers and seasoned veterans. Unlike other how-to books on management, this gem brings to life one man's journey in practical management and leadership excellence. From his explanation of "General Operating Principles" to getting "Back to the Basics," Reggie shares his experiences in this easy-to-read guide for management success.

Having known and worked side by side with Reggie Sykes for nearly twenty years, I can personally say he is a man of integrity with a true passion for giving back. At the very beginning of his book, he provides us with a glimpse into his character by sharing this short but poignant statement: "What you learn, you teach."

In closing, I recommend this book to those entering the management discipline as well as those of us who have been in leadership roles for many years. This book speaks to everyone.

John D. Trent
Senior Director of Strategic Operations
Georgia Ports Authority

Preface

Having recently retired from working in the maritime transportation industry for nearly thirty-nine years, I've come to appreciate a simple rule: "Doing is learning." While I don't know who coined this simple phrase, it has served me well.

In 1971, Sea-Land Service Inc., then the world's largest containerized steamship company, hired me as a management trainee. At the time, Sea-Land had developed and implemented a management-training program that really set the bar for management training in the industry. The training methodology was simple: with proper supervision, the trainees learned on the job. The program was designed to teach by providing them the experience of doing the work and meeting expectations. The departmental supervisors were really manager-teachers: they had the experience of managing their departments while also teaching the trainees.

From the very start of my career, therefore, I came to understand that the sharing of knowledge and skills is a valuable resource, when used by an individual or organization as a tool for growth and learning. Adding value is a fundamental business principle, and shared knowledge and lessons learned are powerful assets and are vital to an organization's success.

Subsequent to working with Sea-Land Service Inc., I worked with Puerto Rico Marine Management Inc. (PRMMI). Sea-Land, the parent company, originally formed PRMMI as an operating company acting as an agent for the Puerto Rican government. As the primary carrier of containerized cargo in the South

American and Caribbean trade lanes, PRMMI offered extensive management opportunities over the years, and so I worked my way up through the ranks. Prior to leaving the organization, I achieved the position of port manager in PRMMI's Jacksonville, Florida, and Charleston, South Carolina, terminals, respectively.

I closed out my career (or, in my words, "finished up") after working sixteen and a half years with the Georgia Ports Authority (GPA), the fourth-largest deepwater port and the second-largest exporting port of containerized cargo in North America. It was during my time at the GPA that I formalized Teachable Points and actively practiced, taught, and shared with many operational staff members the management principles outlined here.

Teachable Points: A Guided Tour for Frontline Supervisors is my way of sharing the knowledge and skills I learned during my nearly thirty-nine years in management. Whether you are an experienced supervisor, a new business owner, a skilled or knowledge worker with supervisory aspirations, or a student about to enter the workforce, it is my hope that you find this book a valuable reference tool.

Chances are, when you scan the topics in the table of contents, you will find nothing "new" there: you'll probably have at least some knowledge of every management concept covered in *Teachable Points*. If you aren't using some of these skill sets now, you may have used them in the past. While the information here isn't new, the presentation and its potential application are. *Teachable Points: A Guided Tour for Frontline Supervisors* validates the fact that my work experience, as presented here, offers operational lessons grounded in basic management principles.

It is important to take notes as you go through *Teachable Points*, and here's why: taking notes as you read this book will help you form your own teachable points. That's right—if you have workplace experience, you have already learned enough to teach. Over time, you likely have established your own best practices, so what you'll share with others are those best practices. You'll teach the lessons you know to be worthy of sharing.

You see, knowledge is not meant to be a private resource. The value of knowledge is realized best when it is shared. So here is a little golden nugget for you: when you share your knowledge and experience, you'll achieve inner fulfillment. You'll come to appreciate that when your efforts actually make a difference in your work environment and beyond, you feel good. And so you'll make those efforts with vigor—not just for those around you, but also for yourself.

Introduction

Teachable Points are based on experience learning, which is good for you and good for your organization. Teachable Points are learned lessons, shared. In this case they are lessons learned while managing, *but the concept is applicable to all endeavors of learning.*

Teachable Points do not constitute an academic exercise. Certainly academic learning is good and has its place. It's about learning to think a problem through, or learning the steps required to do a skill—quite necessary for learning. The Teachable Points concept, however, is about learning in the context of the work you do. I call it "action learning"—learning from your day-to-day, on-the-job work experience.

Action learning is the same as training. And training simply means practicing in order to do something better, learning a skill—not just learning the steps to perform a skill, but learning how to *effectively execute* the steps necessary to proficiently perform that skill. Effective training validates the value of your efforts, and it always produces positive, observable results.

With all that said, here are the key concepts behind Teachable Points:

- Teachable Points is about cascading your learned knowledge to those around you—your learning starts with you, but what you learn must not end with you.

- What you learn about business management should become your teachable points, targeted to those around you.
- Teachable Points is a knowledge-sharing practice.
- Teachable Points is your tool—and a tool is used to get a job done. As a good frontline supervisor, you must always use this tool.

The Teachable Points concept begins with the value of experience learning for an individual or organization.

The idea behind Teachable Points is that a workplace is also a learning place. While Teachable Points are not academic exercises, they promote learning through the experience of being responsible for the use and effective deployment of resources, learning through meeting specific demands in order to produce an acceptable outcome. With experience learning, the major focus is on meeting expectations. That is the big learning point of experience: getting done what is expected.

It is important to understand that operational experience facilitates progressive learning; as you gain experience, you also increase your performance capability. What you experience today is the platform you will stand on tomorrow, and the platform you stand on tomorrow will be improved and more productive than the one you're standing on today—but only if your efforts today move you closer to your potential. Here is a generally accepted life principle to consider: the decisions you make today can influence the quality of your future. You see, as you improve your performance, you are striving to reach your potential with the belief that you're getting closer and closer to it. Striving to reach your potential means you can achieve more if you put forth your best effort each and every day. *Making your best effort is a must.* In the process, you will also gain functional knowledge in your field that you can teach others. It's my perspective that lessons learned through personal experience become hardwired—that is, they're manifested in what I call "instinctive feedback," by which you actively practice lessons learned through your experience.

With the knowledge gained through experience, you are more likely to consistently perform your duties well, and you will always perform better and better—*that's hardwired.* Here is a significant aspect of the Teachable Points concept: if you can appreciate the value of experience, then you also will appreciate the value of sharing lessons learned, the value of teaching. Appreciating your own knowledge and skills will inspire you not only to teach, but also to pay attention to those around you as they share and teach from their own experiences and lessons learned. Stated simply, Teachable Points is a powerful method of operational learning that creates a teaching-learning feedback loop.

Teachable points are a valuable human resources tool, simply because experience, if used effectively, can enhance growth opportunities for an organization's workforce. The experiences that lead to teachable points usually have been cleaned up over time; nonproductive ideas have been weeded out, leaving practicable lessons that are known to be reliable and productive—good stuff to know, use, and share. You see, learning and teaching are complementary HR assets. Through teaching we add value to others, while through learning we receive added value from others. These functions support each other and have the potential to strengthen your performance and the performance of your organization. One without the other means there is more that could have been accomplished in an organization focused on learning. Simply put, learning from others is an efficient method of transferring knowledge and skill, and it must be encouraged by all those with supervisory responsibilities. Know this: if an organization fails to harness its HR assets of learning and teaching, then it certainly and perhaps unknowingly will have lost an opportunity to outperform its competitors.

A teachable moment is an event that is worthy of notice and can benefit those who tap into its value. It is the same with Teachable Points: when they are shared, lessons learned from experience can become valuable building blocks in a career. In fact, Teachable Points fit the definition of *teachable moments*—they are events worthy of notice (for all), they add value to the people who tap into the event, and they facilitate whatever those people are working to accomplish. Keep in mind that experience progressively grows knowledge and skill level in an operational learning environment that focuses on learning and teaching. An effective frontline supervisor's obligation is to actively practice lessons taught by experience.

In a Nutshell: The Value of Experience Learning

The Teachable Points concept is about the value of sharing knowledge. *Teachable Points: A Guided Tour for Frontline Supervisors* connects the principles of learning and teaching. Learning and growth are essential parts of any business. That is why it is critical to appreciate the value of shared knowledge.

I offer my mind-set here on appreciating the value of sharing what experience teaches and what you must come to understand about sharing. You see the starting point for sharing lessons learned is to believe strongly that:

"Your learning starts with you but must not end with you."
- ➢ There's value in learning from your day-to-day experiences.

"What you learn, you teach."
- ➢ Cascade the knowledge you learned from experience to those around you.
- ➢ Teach from the inside.

"You see, knowledge is not a private thing. The value of knowledge is realized best when it is shared."
- ➢ Learn from the experiences of those around you.
- ➢ Learn from the outside.

Your knowledge and experience must not be tacit—you know, only in your head. If your knowledge is tacit, what you have learned cannot be transmitted explicitly to others, so you can't find ways to "show your stuff." Tacit knowledge is useful, but it limits you. It hinders your outreach opportunities, and it minimizes the positive influence you can have on others. That is why you, the frontline supervisor, must learn to share your knowledge with others through both your words and your actions. The first step is to have confidence in your skill level. With confidence, you'll find yourself instinctively reaching out to others, looking for opportunities to share. If you are a frontline supervisor, you must know your job and be good at it. To be good at your job, you must always strive to excel in your areas or responsibilities and take pride in your work. Aiming for excellence is the key. You see, you must be willing to stay focused on your personal growth and commit quality time and significant effort to developing subject-matter expertise in your field.

By the way, your subordinates will expect you to be good at performing your duties, for they understand the impact your personal performance can have on them and what they can accomplish. We'll discuss the concept of meeting and exceeding expectations throughout *Teachable Points*, but for now just remember that your subordinates will have certain expectations of you, and they will be observing your leadership skills constantly as they assess your personal performance. That is what makes your knowledge, and how you display it, a valuable tool in the workplace or any other learning environment. To believe or behave otherwise—acting as if knowledge is private and should not be displayed for others to observe and learn from—only limits what can be accomplished in the workplace or in other areas where learning enriches the environment. If what's in your head stays in your head, you have devalued a priceless tool—your experiences and lessons learned.

Sharing what you know with others is a tool that can slingshot you and your organization into a best-in-class industry position. You see, knowledge stimulates individual creativity, and shared knowledge can exponentially broaden the creative thinking of an organization. While there is no doubt that sharing what you have learned is a personal choice, your best choice as a manager is to share. So what you learn, you teach. If you have proven the value of your skills and your workplace performance has been generally recognized as inspirational by those around you, what you can do now is show others the ropes and display your skills. Once your knowledge has been recognized as a productive and reliable resource, it becomes valuable. Valued knowledge is easy to share, because those around you will aggressively seek opportunities to tap into your subject-matter expertise. They probably will be impressed by your skills and invigorated by how you perform your supervisory duties. Then your subordinates, peers, and others in your group will be pushed not only to improve their performance, which may enhance their personal growth opportunities, but also to appreciate the value of displaying their own skills. Observing the good work of others is exciting and can bake enthusiasm into the attitudes of all those around you, including your staff, because people just like to see good results attributable to good effort.

Your contribution is simply your willingness to share. Knowledge is a powerful tool, but if it is not shared, its value is diminished. So don't keep it in your head, as if it were your personal property or for your exclusive use. In business, the primary goal is to add value to what you have, and sharing your knowledge and skills adds value and contributes to a learning-rich environment, which adds further value to your organization. Your willingness to share, therefore, is the key to successfully linking teaching and learning, which together contribute greatly to your personal success and the success of others around you.

Later in this book, when we discuss communication, you'll come to understand that the listener—the person to whom a message is directed—is actually the communicator. If the intended message is not received, communication has not happened. So when you share your knowledge, you are actually communicating. But communication is contingent on your intended message being received by the relevant individual, group, or department. My point is this: when sharing your knowledge as the subject-matter expert, it is important to do so with humility, while clearly indicating that what you are sharing (teaching) is in the interest of the individual, group, or department. You are sharing your knowledge and skills for the benefit of everyone in your work environment, not to boost your self-esteem or reputation, or for other selfish reasons.

1

General Operating Principles

a) The Purpose of the Frontline Supervisor
b) Effective Management and Use of Resources
c) The Work Process
d) Plan—Do—Check—Act (PDCA)
e) Personnel
f) Employee Satisfaction
g) Equipment
h) Safety
i) Your Personal Performance—Your Personal Goals

The Purpose of the Frontline Supervisor

As a frontline supervisor, your purpose is to meet and exceed expectations. To do so, you must first clearly understand what you are charged with accomplishing. Start by answering three very important questions:

- What is my role as a frontline supervisor?
- What are my responsibilities?
- What does the organization expect of me?

First, the frontline supervisory position is always linked to the products or services the organization offers; the position connects the organization's production or service strategy to those actually performing the work. The frontline supervisor must also ensure that the output of all products or services in his/her charge meets specifications and is consistently within acceptable tolerance levels as defined by the customer and agreed to by the organization. One of the frontline supervisor's highest priorities, therefore, is directing subordinates to perform their tasks with skill accurately. In order to do this, the supervisor must have a clear and thorough understanding of the work processes. That is, he or she must know how the work is done; how to effectively lead those performing the work at each step of the business processes in his/her charge; and how to effectively and efficiently utilize resources.

Effective frontline supervisors must understand how their job fits into the work their organization does and the commitments it has made to its customers. The frontline supervisor can be effective in meeting those commitments by understanding the value of excellence in four key areas:

- quality service
- effectiveness
- process efficiency
- personal performance

These are the focus of four management principles you may already have encountered or will encounter during your career. The question is, how do you handle them?

- *Quality service* is delivering a service and/or product meeting the customer's standards within tolerance levels over time. Consistency is a critical factor in defining an organization's performance and its ability to reliably provide a product or service that conforms to its customers' demands.
- *Effectiveness* is meeting service commitments and promises made to the customer. It means knowing

where your customer wants you to go and that a properly executed plan will get you there.
- *Efficiency* is using resources well and eliminating waste. In the context of business, *waste* is using resources but gaining less than what was expected or hoped for—or, in some cases, gaining nothing at all. Internal efficiencies directly benefit your organization but must not remain within the boundaries of your organization. Operating efficiencies must extend beyond those boundaries to positively impact your customers. Through customer-focused, cocreative business-process initiatives, an organization can (1) establish good customer relationships; (2) minimize nonproductive customer demands disguised as customer service; and (3) establish what matters most to the customer. Allowing the customer to have input into, or at least see, your internal work process will positively influence the customer's evaluation of services delivered.
- *Personal performance.* There are two levels of *personal performance*: potential and actual. Your potential performance level is the highest level you can achieve; your actual performance level is the current level of your achievement. You should always know the gap between these two levels and be working to narrow it. One way to gauge the gap is to regularly evaluate the results of your work. You must realize that your performance can always be better, so the question you must constantly ask yourself and answer honestly is "Could I have done better?" Just for the record, the correct answer is yes—but that answer has value only if you clearly define what could have been done better and take action to eliminate or at least minimize the reasons the performance falls short of your capabilities. Performing below what you are capable of must be considered waste—*not by others, but by you.*

The entire management team must practice these important principles in order to achieve the value that they can produce for any organization. In other words, these are collective business principles: *all supervisors and management staff must adhere to these principles, all four of them, to near-perfection.* These principles apply not just to you, but also to everyone in your organization. Together you are equal to more, and can produce more, than your individual efforts. That's not an original statement, but it's certainly a proven fact.

Providing Quality Service

The delivery of quality service or a quality product must be the first objective of any organization wishing to achieve profitability and sustainability. It is important to understand, however, that any operation or business process must be aligned with the overall strategic plan of the organization. A successful business strategy must deliver a quality of service that yields these sustainable results:

- Customer retention: your customers see no need to seek the services of your competition.
- Customer loyalty: your customers are willing to tell others about your product or service while continuing to be customers you can count on.
- Proper return on spending: your customer-focused internal efficiency equals profit.

This strategy should apply to every department and every subgroup within it. It also applies to the task or functions of a frontline supervisor, who's responsible for delivering a service that complements the commitments made by the organization. Maintaining customer focus and operating efficiency is how a frontline supervisor delivers these three objectives, which are essential to the success of an organization.

Teachable Points

Keep in mind that quality is just as important in the service industry as it is in the manufacturing industry. Performance is measurable in both, but in the service industry you must be a little more creative to develop meaningful measures. It's easier to validate units produced per man-hour than it is to measure customers' willingness to promote your service, or to determine whether they find it easy to do business with your organization.

In providing your service, you must understand that the customer is the heartbeat of your organization, and effective frontline supervision is what keeps the beat steady and stable. Quality service is built on meeting the customer's *needs* and *requirements*—but it's important to understand the difference between the two business principles. As explained by George Eckes,[1] an expert in the Six Sigma methodology, meeting the customer's *needs* means having the infrastructure to establish and maintain a viable business relationship, while meeting the customer's *requirements* means having the ability to deliver the customer's critical wants. By meeting both, you keep your customer happy and validate your organization's effectiveness. You must always remember this important, generally accepted business principle: the customer defines the quality of service delivered based on what he or she actually sees. That is not to say that the customers' evaluation of an organization's performance is always correct, but it is their evaluation that really matters, and that's the bottom line. That is why quality service is your direct link to your customer and is what seals a viable long-term business relationship.

The key for the frontline supervisor is to see what the customer sees: those things that fall short of what he or she expects. The question is, do you recognize those shortfalls? Do you see them from your customers' perspective? Because that's the perspective you must use to identify the critical steps in your processes and measure and monitor their outcome. Measuring and monitoring them can give you a heads-up about potential shortfalls and the opportunity to take corrective action before the product or service is delivered to the customer. If you do not see your performance and the quality of your service from your customer's perspective while you are delivering that service, you certainly will if and when the business goes away. Keep in mind that service shortfalls are not intangible. Tangible things happen to your customers when your service fails to meet expectations: more cost, longer cycle times, service failure to their customers, and possibly the loss of their customers. Here is an important fact: service delivered must be acceptable to the customer. There is no discomfort from the customer's perspective when your performance consistently meets that standard. Dissatisfaction surfaces when the customer sees and feels a quality of service that is delivered in an unacceptable manner and that fails to meet critical requirements and specifications.

And what do customers expect? Believe it or not, they expect perfect performance. They expect whatever you give them—service or product—to be flawless. And that expectation is not unreasonable, for in the context of customer service, *flawless* just means performance in excess of what is expected. If your customers are willing to pay for products and services provided by you and your organization, they want them to be flawless. If your organization cannot deliver flawless service, how can your customers deliver flawless service to *their* customers? Requiring flawlessness is not demanding too much; it is just expecting a proper return on spending. After all, flawless performance is what you should expect from any primary supplier or vendor you do business with.

Effective Management and Use of Resources

There are three primary elements critical to achieving a high level of business performance. The first element is your work process. This is the driving force of doing your work efficiently and cannot be overstated, as will be clearly manifested throughout *Teachable Points*. The second element is your personnel—without a doubt one of your most powerful business resources, and the key to internal operating efficiencies.

And then there is the third element, your equipment. It is vitally important to have the right tools and equipment. If you hope to run an efficient operation, those tools and equipment must be available and, once deployed, must be reliable. Systems must be in place to prevent damaged equipment or equipment needing maintenance services off-line. Deploying damaged or poorly functioning equipment is a constraint to productivity that is preventable. A good frontline supervisor strives diligently to minimize or eliminate constraints and avoid preventable equipment failures. It is also critically important to ensure that all employees are properly trained and qualified to operate the equipment safely.

In order to achieve a high level of performance, you must understand that these three elements of management—work process, personnel, and equipment—are independent functions. However, the performance of each element can affect the outcome you're working to achieve, and so to that degree they are interconnected and even interdependent. Imagine having a good work process and proper use of your equipment resources but poor personnel management.

In fact, imagine any combination of two good elements and one bad element: what you get is an outcome that is less than near-perfect. Taken together, these business elements are multiplicative: independent variables but part of the same process, which in statistical terms is defined as Rolled Throughput Yield (RTY). Imagine that your work process is performed at 90% yield (efficiency), and your personnel management is performed at 90% yield. You would calculate the RTY for these two elements by multiplying them: 90% x 90% = 81% RTY. If your equipment yield is also at 90%, then you would calculate the RTY of the three by factoring that variable in, too: 81% x 90% = 72.9%.

Working with these three elements at 90% yield each, without making any changes or improvements, means that the probability of doing all three correctly or at a 100% yield is only 72.9%. You see, these elements are complementary; they build upon each other. So operating with each of these critical elements at 90% efficiency is significantly less than near-perfect. The measurable gap between an average of 90% and an RTY of 72.9% is best described as waste—and the bigger the gap, the more waste. Simply put, capability not achieved is waste.

The Work Process

Remember that your work process is a resource. It directly influences the quality of your work and has a measurable impact on customer satisfaction. In fact, it's an open secret that better efficiency and increased productivity begin with your work process. As a frontline supervisor, you must ensure that an excellent work process is designed and implemented for all your assignments and tasks. Whenever you review a process that you own as a provider of services or products to the next step in that process, identify the constraints that have the most influence on a successful outcome. You must always strive to control those influential factors that have a direct correlation to efficiency and productivity. The frontline supervisor's job is to either eliminate or strengthen any such factors found when reviewing or evaluating the work. The benefits of an excellent business process are twofold: first, it enhances your internal efficiencies and therefore your cost-saving opportunities, and second, it ensures a viable, sustainable business relationship with your customers.

What is a work process, anyway? It is the series of steps you take to perform a task that requires the input of resources. The

Teachable Points

process adds value to the input by creating a product or service for the end user, the customer. And by design, a business process can minimize rework, remove constraints to productivity, and, even more important, allow you to do more with less. The purpose of a work process is to produce a favorable output or service outcome, but remember that the outcome must be favorable to the customer, the end user. If you want to produce excellent outcomes, you first must accept ownership of the business processes in your charge. You then must make sure that an excellent work process is set up for all your tasks. Even if you didn't design your current work processes, you certainly have the responsibility, as the process owner, to redesign them if they allow for failure, defects, or shortfalls. The key is to know the outcome of your current work processes. Is rework ever necessary? Is the cycle time too long? Is the customer satisfied? You must identify from your customer's perspective the critical steps in your processes and measure their outcome. Your goal is to ensure that any business process in your charge is not just capable but also acceptable, allowing for highly efficient performance.

Improving your work process requires constant effort; it's an effort that is never finished, because you should never be satisfied with what you have or where you are. You must continually review your work, because if you do, it is likely that you will always find ways to improve it. An improved process may even require less input, or the input may remain the same while your output increases. You can always find opportunities to use your resources more efficiently while also improving the quality of services delivered to your customers. There must not be any limits to improving a process; if there were, they would be self-imposed, and an indication that you think there is no more to be gained. Such an attitude is baseless and must not be allowed to prevail among a frontline supervisor and his/her subordinates.

Before you can make any process improvements, you have to know how you are doing and whether any improvements are necessary (and they usually are). To know how you are doing, you must measure your outcomes daily, weekly, and monthly. Just make sure that your system of measurement is appropriate. It should indicate how well you are keeping your commitments to your customers and whether you are meeting internal efficiencies standards. You know the old saying, "What gets measured gets done"? That old saying is true, but only if you are measuring the right things correctly.

Stay away from measuring trivial things—you know, things that don't positively affect quality or efficiency and that offer few or no benefits. An effective measurement system gives you feedback in time to identify the cause of potential failures, defects, or shortfalls and facilitates development and implementation of viable solutions. Know this: your customers measure your performance. So by effectively monitoring your own work by regularly measuring the output of your efforts, you will likely avoid falling short of the standards your customer expects—and better yet, you may exceed them. Here is a question you must know the answer to: Is there a gap between the quality that you promise (or that your customers expect) and the quality you actually deliver? The answer to any honest evaluation is likely to be yes. So your focus must be to define specific actions that will close the gap and then implement them as improvement initiatives. Implementing a combination of appropriate measures, including constant customer feedback, is a pretty good way to pinpoint any gap in the level of service provided. Paying attention to what customers say to you and monitoring their feedback about the quality of your work is an effective method of measuring their assessment of your efforts.

Plan—Do—Check—Act
The Shewhart-Deming (PDCA) Cycle

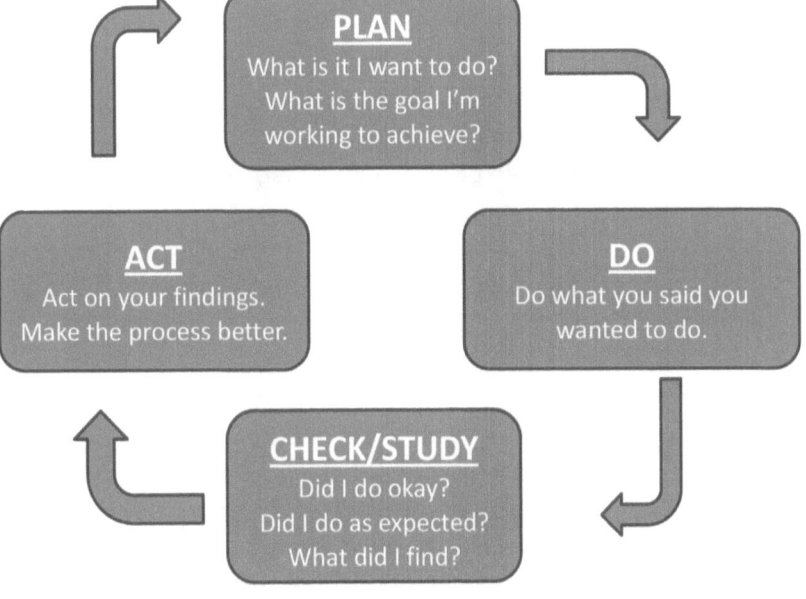

Plan—Do—Check—Act (PDCA)

PDCA is a structured method for maintaining a continuous process of improvement. It ensures that a work process reflects any changes in your business conditions or circumstances, and it quantifies your current work performance. PDCA is a tool developed by two gurus in the area of quality: Dr. Walter A. Shewhart and Dr. W. Edwards Deming.[2]

PDCA is a quality control tool that is very effective. While it is not new, it is certainly a proven and highly functional tool that is used by many successful organizations today, especially those that have implemented a Six Sigma program. Take a look at the PDCA map. It really is an easy-to-follow graphic view of the flow of improving a business process.

When using the PDCA improvement methodology, you always follow these steps:

Plan: Ask, *What am I working to accomplish, and have I identified the opportunity or the problems?*
Do: Execute the plan. If what you're doing now looks okay, ask, *Have I exploited the opportunity or fixed the problem, and could I have done better?* (The answer should always be yes.)
Check: Ask, *How did I do? By adjusting a few steps, will the production process be even better?* (Yes.)
Act: Make the adjustments, monitor the process, and go back to Plan.

PDCA is the heartbeat of any serious continuous improvement initiative. At some point in Dr. Deming's analysis of the PDCA methodology, he substituted the *check* (C) with *study* (S); he reasoned that when you are checking, you are really studying the results of your actions to understand what may have caused the need to make adjustments to the work process. In other words, he inserted the necessary element of learning into the cycle.[3]

On a continuing basis you must communicate your work process to your peers and other participants involved in the same business process. Those who are affected by what you do should have some knowledge about what you do. Keep in mind that your connection with others is part of an integrated work flow that crosses departmental boundaries. It's a normal course of conducting business—"cross-functional collaboration" is a good way to say it. You, your subordinates, and others involved in the process must actively practice the "must do" business principle of cross-functional collaboration. One step in the process always feeds the next, which likely will be handled in another area or department, and by several people. So effectively connecting your work in a process with the next operational or transactional step is the single best way to minimize or eliminate the need for fire-damage control, which usually is assignable to breakdowns between steps in the process or an uncoordinated transfer of input resources from one step to the next.

Remember, there is a downside to fire-damage-control measures: they yield only minor results, if that, and they do not last. Plus, by the time you implement them, the damage is done. Symptoms of the root problem may go away for a while, but the problem remains and surely will recur—at which point you must go back into the damage-control mode again. Fire-damage control is usually the result of missed or poorly executed critical steps in a business process, so effective cross-functional communication is the best way to keep the damage-control team off the field and out of the game. The idea is to fix the step or steps that allowed the failure, defect, or shortfall to happen.

Frontline supervisors must not let fire damage-control become a part of their daily routine, always working the hottest problem-of-the-day instead of the next priority. If there's a fire, they must find its root cause. An effective analysis of the current process can determine what step(s) caused the fire or allowed it to occur. Once that determination is made, those steps can be improved or the constraining factor eliminated.

That's why it's important to have open communications across departmental or functional boundaries. You must know what your peers and others need from you, why and when they need it—and, more important, the negative impact if you fail to deliver properly to the next step. It's important to realize that none of your work assignments starts or ends with you. It is very important to understand that your performance and how you contribute to the performance of others is a critical factor in the workplace, right where you are. Always seek to share with your peers and others any best practices and lessons you've learned; if you don't, you'll lose an opportunity to continually improve. Inter-function or inter-task communication is informative and better connects you with your work environment. If you know what is happening around you, you're less likely to unnecessarily adjust procedures or make changes that adds no value to your work. The goal of inter-function or inter-task communication is to prevent delays, cost increases, failures in customer service, and the wasteful use of valuable resources.

Stated simply, the objective of any business process is to perform and deliver to the customer as efficiently as possible. If you don't actively practice inter-function or inter-task communication, you and those in your group will become firefighters. Fighting fires will keep you working, but you'll be working on fixing problems, which creates waste. So the key to *minimizing the need for constant* fire-damage control is to establish solid business processes that are both capable and stable and ensure an acceptable outcome for your efforts and those of your subordinates. You see, effective firefighting means planning not to have a fire. An excellent work process that is under continuous review will prevent a constant wave of sudden emergencies requiring you to continually reactivate fire-damage-control measures.

Personnel

Your personnel are among your most valuable resources and clearly an investment in producing your desired outcome. More important, your people are the one distinguishing factor between your organization and its competitors. All other factors can be evenly balanced if your competitors choose to invest equally in infrastructure and deployment of resources. They may have the capability to match your organization in all functional areas, but what they cannot match is your people. So the acknowledgment that your people are your most valuable resource must be defined as a "core value."

Employees with longevity usually are very knowledgeable, well-informed, and highly skilled. As a good frontline supervisor, you must know who those employees are and what they can contribute to your operation, and then find ways to use their productive attributes and those of all subordinates. It's the smart thing to do: each employee has something to give, and many want to give, so let them give. There is no better way for you to facilitate, and for them to achieve and actively practice, intrinsic motivation (or as I call it, "self-generated enthusiasm"). Remember one thing, however: intrinsic motivation has its own engine—*the individual.*

Always let your subordinates cascade their knowledge on you by sharing their teachable points. Your subordinates have knowledge, and their knowledge has value, but only if you use it. You see, your personnel should be a resource that produces value, not a resource that consumes resources and adds no value. If a subordinate has knowledge and a high skill level and you don't use them, then you are wasting, overriding, and devaluing a powerful human resource. In the maritime industry, a ship consumes fuel, but it also takes cargo to the subsequent port, and so the fuel consumption produces a favorable economic impact in that port community. A good frontline supervisor will tap into his subordinates' resources (their knowledge and skills) and as a result will likely always produce a favorable outcome. It is very difficult to satisfy your direct customer contact if you fail to tap into and properly utilize the value of the internal resources assignable to you, including your subordinates.

Employee Satisfaction

We've talked about the importance of process and the fact that a satisfied employee is more likely to keep a process on track and moving at the right speed. A process can be on track but moving at the wrong speed, and then you get run over. Stuff happens, defects show up, shortfalls happen, rework must be done. You will find yourself doing the same things over and over and over again. Using the knowledge and skills of your subordinates will go a long way toward keeping a process on track, as it's likely that their functional knowledge of the work process is quite high. Of course, "on track" means performing at a level that produces an output that fully complies with the organization's commitments and exceeds the customer's expectations. If your subordinates are satisfied with their work and what's expected of them, they will likely make it easier for you to meet and exceed the expectations of your direct customer contact. Their performance can make a positive difference. Opportunities to achieve in the workplace are what will keep your subordinates satisfied and motivated. (In fact, the words *satisfied* and *motivated* are synonymous as used here.)

You see, if your subordinates are knowledgeable about the work process but have no avenue by which to contribute that knowledge, it is reasonable for them to conclude that their knowledge is valueless at work. If you know that your professional knowledge has value that is not recognized in your workplace, you would obviously be disheartened. So it is critically important to identify those who have a high skill level, and in a reasonable way, tap into their skills at critical times. I said earlier that knowledge is not a private thing—and that applies to your subordinates' knowledge, too. In fact, if a subordinate's knowledge is private, it usually is not his/her intent or desire to keep it that way; more often it is private because you failed to accept it or to grasp it, and you chose not to use his or her knowledge. Remember, anytime you miss an opportunity for your subordinates to add value to what you are working to accomplish, you've wasted a productive resource.

Equipment

Your equipment is a resource. The tools you use can impact how you provide service and the quality of that service. Take steps to ensure that all equipment deployed for use is in good working order. After all, any equipment operated by your staff as a function of your assignments is under your jurisdiction. It is therefore your job to ensure that those responsible for equipment maintenance are not practitioners of "breakdown maintenance"—you know, just fixing equipment after it has broken down. Imagine the negative effect that maintenance method would have on your capability to meet acceptable productivity standards.

Training your staff on the proper use of that equipment is the first step in preventing accidents and lost productivity. Proper use also means *no faster than your best safe speed*. When your staff is working in what could be considered an industrial complex, where there is dynamic movement of equipment and people and some components function independently, operating speed becomes critically important. Working at proper speed has the potential to prevent accidents. A sudden emergency is often the first indicator that an accident is imminent. In an industrial environment, an operator working at "best safe speed" has enough time to react to a sudden emergency and is likelier to avoid an accident.

We all know that training is essential for new employees. In this context, training simply means teaching employees how to do things differently, how to perform in what is known to be the best way to achieve at a higher level. Your subordinates may have good equipment operating skills, but it is important that their skills fit their new environment. Training and observation can make their transition to your work environment smooth. Observation for proper use is a preventive action. If you observe improper use, do not let it go uninterrupted.

Reporting equipment problems as a matter of course can be effective in limiting the deployment of damaged or nonfunctioning equipment. So it is imperative to have an inspection procedure in place, properly implemented and monitored by qualified staffers. There must always be a corrective-action plan for failed equipment as well as a solid action plan to ensure timely repair. Imagine going to work without all the proper tools: you might go to work, but there is no way you'll be as productive as you are capable of being. You'll produce less while your input remains the same. The same is true with your equipment: if you don't have all your equipment available and in good order, your crew will be less productive.

Safety

Safety is a strategic mission for many organizations, and its importance must be cascaded to every employee in the organization, including your direct reports. They must understand that a safe work environment is not only productive, but it is every employee's responsibility.

It is important to understand that an unsafe workplace is an unproductive workplace. On the other hand a safe work environment is a major contributing factor to a productive operation. By design, the purpose of a safe work environment is not to inhibit performance standards but rather enhance performance capabilities.

Curtis Foltz, Executive Director of the Georgia Ports Authority, often advises that *"the safest terminal is a closed terminal."* In other words, the dynamics of a fast moving and flexible terminal operation create risk. Conversely, an effective safety program efficiently minimizes risk by eliminating or reducing the conditions that are assignable to unsafe events.

Remember, an effective safety program is a Key Process Input Variable (KPIV) that yields a productive terminal operation that meets internal performance standards. As a result, safety and performance excellence are complementary. So for the frontline supervisor, it's not one or the other you are working to achieve, but rather it's both.

You see, safety is not and must not be designated as "Other Duties as Assigned" to those in your group. It is really a collective obligation. The frontline supervisor is obligated to always seek out conditions that contribute to an unsafe work environment and take immediate, measured steps to minimize or when possible, eliminate those conditions. Once they are minimized or eliminated, the supervisor must take further measured steps designed to keep the new corrective-action plan under control.
It is important to understand that without control measures, unsafe conditions will likely resurface and the dangers of an unsafe environment will again increase the probability of an accident.

The emphasis on safety is nothing new in business and industry today. I think we all can agree, however, that the importance of safety has been elevated in the workplace. Senior staff is now discussing safety by asking more focused questions, such as

- What is the mean time between accidents?
- What is the probability of going xxx (hours—days—weeks) before the next accident?
- What are the three or four most frequent reasons for the occurrence of a certain type of accident?
- Do we have an analysis of accidents caused by resources used or infrastructure design versus our people?

With senior staff's commitment to ensuring a safe workplace for everyone, you will be expected to stay focused on safety and continually improve the results of your safety program. Senior staff focus means that safety is now a major factor in measuring not only your success, but also the success of your organization. So it's important to recognize that in most organizations, the value placed on safety is now at a new level of thinking. Today, it is at its highest level ever.

Your Personal Performance—Your Personal Goals

In evaluating your own work performance, you should generally have two goals in mind: to achieve the business results your organization expects and to earn the opportunity to build a successful career. The path to reaching both of these goals is to focus on your family goals. Everyone has goals for personal achievement, and family is a major component in everyone's life. Building a successful career certainly is not the only thing that contributes to achieving family goals, but it is a major contributor to achieving them; so to achieve your personal goals in employment, you must also stay focused on your family goals. To be successful in your career, you must have functional understanding of this fact.

The late Rev. Freddie Henry Dunn, who was my pastor in my youth, taught us with vigor, "You are what you're becoming." If you want to advance as you build your career, then you must work toward those advancements today—work toward tomorrow's positions today. The strength of the foundation you'll stand on tomorrow depends upon your performance, your dedication, your attitude, and how you execute those personal attributes today. So in the workplace and at home, "you are what you're becoming." Staying focused on such a principle as you work toward your family and performance goals means exercising personal dedication in all that you do.

So how do you do that? If I had to use one word, I'd borrow the core principle of Coastal Logistic Group Inc., a third-party logistics company in Savannah, Georgia: *diligence*. Diligence means giving your very best effort in all that you do. By being diligent, you always make deliberate, well-reasoned choices. Diligence is about outcome, about advancing your opportunities for personal achievement while contributing to the performance of your organization. It means taking an honest look at what and how you are doing in the important areas in your life, including your work life, and when necessary making adjustments that are positive and fulfilling.

Diligence is a straight line to achieving positive results. In addition, what you are working to achieve ultimately benefits you. No doubt your organization benefits if you are dedicated to advancing; in the end, though, your advancement is mutually beneficial. High-level personal performance means that your company is okay, and you're okay. And that is a good thing.

2

Frontline Supervision: A Challenging Position

Those of us who have been where you are today know that frontline supervision can be—and usually is—a dynamic, fluid, very active position with many challenges. The question is, how do you respond to those challenges? While they may be uninvited, you will surely face them in a business environment. In fact, given the dynamics of business, challenges are inherent—and that introduces a degree of difficulty. Remember that your management team and senior management staff know and understand the degree of difficulty you face each day. Without a doubt, many of your senior staffers have been where you are now. It is important to understand, however, that frontline supervision is not just an entry-level position. All management levels are close enough to affect the customer. So if you are close enough to influence the customer, for better or worse, then you qualify as a frontline supervisor. Every day, frontline supervision can affect how customers evaluate performance—not just your personal performance, but the performance of your organization.

Let's discuss the challenges you'll face in the context of a sports metaphor. We'll use the sport of gymnastics and score two floor routines:

> The first routine—Round off with a back handspring, double back somersault in a tuck position: an 8.0 is the

highest score you can achieve, but *only if you stick the landing*.

The second routine—Round off with a back handspring, double back somersault in a layout position with a full twist: a 10.0 is the highest score you can achieve, but again, *only if you stick the landing*.

This degree of difficulty is a challenge that you must accept and meet if you want to be competitive in the sport of gymnastics. So you practice, because that's what you must do to excel in the sport of gymnastics. There is always something new in the sport—your competition stiffens, or a newly developed maneuver is introduced—so your training is never really finished. If you do stop training, you'll no longer be competitive in the sport. Last year's compulsory and optional routines are not competitive in today's competition. It's the same with frontline supervision: to be an effective frontline supervisor, you must turn learning into a practice sport. In supervising, as in gymnastics, training is continuous. And in supervising, as in gymnastics, with continuous training you'll learn how to stick your landing.

When you practice a sport, you pay attention to the results of your efforts. It is the same with frontline supervision: when you're working to exceed what is expected of you, you must pay attention to the results of your efforts. When you monitor your efforts and their results, you will probably identify some things that need to be fixed. Your job is to identify those problems, analyze their impact, determine their root cause(s), and fix whatever shortfalls or defects you find in the process. Next, focus on eliminating or at least minimizing any constraints, and then take measures to control the improved process. You will see better results, and your efforts will more consistently exceed expectations.

Here is a little golden nugget that can help make you more comfortable in your workplace: humor makes the work environment a pleasant place to be. It positions you to handle the double back somersault with a full twist and even stick the landing—no extra steps taken. Humor is a very powerful emotion. It relaxes you. And when you're relaxed, you're in a better position to handle the stresses and challenges of your job.

You see, the frontline supervisor's challenges require a bit of a balancing act, as there are shifting forces coming at you from more than one direction. Your direct supervisor will pull you one way. Your subordinates will pull you another way. And your customer will pull you every which way but loose (and sometimes that way, too). A good balancing act requires *dynamic stability*. This phrase may seem contradictory, but really it isn't. It simply means dealing with the ebb and flow of your business processes and procedures both effectively and efficiently. Here's how you do that:

- *Flexibility:* There is nothing wrong with being strong in a position. It is important, though, to know how to protect your position while handling shifting circumstances and still taking care of your customer's requirements. By giving thought to why shifting circumstances are occurring, you can be reasonably flexible about a procedure or process while still meeting the customer's expectations and remaining effective and efficient in matters of cost. Such shifts are to be expected in business, and so it is incumbent that you make any adjustments to your process in a way that resolves the problem without compromising your commitment to your customers. "Customer first" is a winning strategy that must always be your first priority, but an effective business strategy also follows a parallel track, a commitment to efficiency in internal operations. You should follow not one track or the other, but both.

Teachable Points

- *Adaptability:* Sometimes a major shift in your work processes and procedures is required. A significant change in the customer's requirements, your organization's commitments, or your competitor's actions may mean redesigning how you do your work in order to meet your customer's requirements and remain competitive. You must understand that over time, circumstances will shift. So you must adapt to the changing business environment by making process changes that are customer-focused while still fully compliant with internal operating efficiency standards.

However, you must be consistent when exercising flexibility or adapting to dynamic circumstances. Remember, customizing a business process is not a bad thing if it is done in a way that takes care of the customer and your organization. Customizing can be easy and sometimes even very complex. So when navigating through these various levels of business-process adjustments, it is appropriate to be thorough in your analysis of the conditions driving the need to make major changes in your current processes and procedures. The goal is to make sure that any solutions implemented to mitigate significant customer service matters are directed at the root causes(s) and not at their symptoms or at minor problems that are easy to resolve. Always remember that the desired outcome is for the customer to be okay, and for your organization to be okay, too.

Service: The Purpose of Business

In defining the purpose of business, you first must answer two questions. The first is what is the purpose of *your* business? The answer is service. The second is what is the purpose of *your customer's* business? Again, the answer is service. The bottom line is this: successfully serving *your* customers positions them to successfully serve *their* customers and to be a competitive force in their industry.

As a frontline supervisor, you must have a functional understanding that the purpose of business is *service*: the quality of the service you deliver, as a function of your organization, depends upon your personal performance. There are three generally accepted principles that you must be cognizant of and factor into your supervisory philosophy:

1. Reliability: Deliver on time, every time, and in full compliance with the Critical to Quality (CTQ) requirements of your customer.
2. Responsiveness: Make proficient and prompt delivery of requested services or questions about service transactions.
3. Flexibility: Be quick to resolve problems or handle unexpected events, including changes in the business process or in the customer's service requirements.

Teachable Points

With these three business principles in mind, a frontline supervisor can, to a degree, impact the outcome of the customer's business. That's an important fact to remember, especially if you and your organization serve as your customer's primary provider of a product or service; service providers are important, but in many ways they are interchangeable. If your organization doesn't provide good service—if it isn't reliable, responsive, and flexible—then your organization is liable to be replaced, and quickly. Truckers, rail operators, brokers, freight forwarders, agents, and almost all vendors can be replaced with just a phone call or two.

As a primary service provider, remember that your organization's commitment to your customer is like a promise—you're giving your word. You're saying, "Trust me," but in a special way. You see, personal trust often comes before you've proven yourself trustworthy. But in business, you must prove that your service is trustworthy first, and then you must prove yourself again with every service event. Therefore the principle focus of the frontline supervisor and his/her organization is delivering service at a level of quality that consistently exceeds promises made. Here is what you'll hear from your direct customer contacts regarding the quality of service you deliver: "Show me. Show me again. Show me again. Show me again." That message aligns with a very popular saying in the Total Quality Management circle: "Doing the right thing the right way, the first time and every time." Boy, they are just a few words, but they have so much meaning, and an impact that can significantly influence the success of an organization. The frontline supervisor must come to understand how important it is to get the job done right, just as the expression says.

4

Customers and Their Expectations

a) Getting and Keeping the Customer
b) Being On Point
c) Service Commitment
d) Predictably Unpredictable
e) Service and Yesterday's Value
f) Concentric Circles

Marketing and sales are charged with "getting the customer"; the operation group is charged with "keeping the customer." To keep the customer, operations must deliver a level of service that the *customer* considers valuable. It is a primary business principle that value is defined by the customer, from his/her point of view. You do not commit to quality service for your own purpose; you commit to quality service for the customer's purpose. That positions you to fulfill your purpose and your organization's purpose: *service.*

Remember the motto from Bill Clinton's 1992 presidential campaign—"It's the economy, stupid"? Well, for you and your organization, "It's the customer, stupid." Forgive the blunt language, but it was a winning strategy then. In today's business environment, there's no use sugarcoating the harsh reality of tough competition.

Keeping the customer satisfied requires more than just rhetoric—talk is cheap. As an operator, you are responsible for transforming talk into reality. Your work is more about doing than talking. You keep the customer through your actions and how you go about meeting his/her requirements. In any business operation, a good work process is one of the most important drivers to consistently meeting customers' requirements and keeping them happy and satisfied. "It is the customer, stupid" is not a complicated initiative, so don't make it complicated by shifting your focus away from your customers. Given that they set the requirements and performance standards you must meet, you must understand that they will be dissatisfied and not tolerate service below those standards, and the last thing you want as a frontline supervisor is for your customer to take corrective action because of poor performance. You must and can prevent such an outcome by clearly understanding the value of service and how the customer perceives your efforts on his/her behalf.

If a customer is dissatisfied with a service event or transaction, think of it as a negative response to a survey question. Remember, your goal is to meet the standard of *near-perfect*, meaning there will be opportunities—although hopefully not many—to resolve service events that displease the customer. When facing customer dissatisfaction, never forget that responsiveness is the key: process or performance failures that lead to customer dissatisfaction must be resolved immediately. Of course, the goal is to have no complaints, but when there is a complaint, you have an excellent opportunity to demonstrate your interest in your customer. Here is how to address a complaint:

- Tell the customer what measures will be taken to resolve the problem.
- Make sure corrective actions are effective and implemented quickly.
- Include control measures in the solution, and make sure those measures are monitored internally, locked into

the review process, and clearly communicated to the customer.

Getting and Keeping the Customer

To keep your customers, you must know what they expect, and your performance must exceed their expectations. For the frontline supervisor, the simplest way to approach this begins with the words *what* and *how*: *What* do your customers expect of you and your organization as priorities, and *how* can you and your organization deliver those priorities? It may be a simple formula—but boy, is it an important one. As a frontline supervisor, you will be dealing with your direct customer contacts (DCC) on a daily basis. So it is important that your DCCs communicate to you exactly what they expect, what will fully meet their demand for service. Knowing what the customer wants is critical, so if your DCC does not clearly advise you of his/her requirements and specifications, you must initiate the communication and then listen carefully to what the customer is saying. Customers' impression of your organization starts with you, so your performance must be at a level that keeps the customer attracted to the product or service offered by your organization.

You must constantly be cognizant of the fact that customers are evaluating your performance and whether you are meeting or exceeding their expectations. Here are a few factors your customers will evaluate continually: quality of service, promptness, reliability, ease of doing business, responsiveness, compliance with specifications, and, of course, price. While price is an important "what," it is critical that you deliver other attributes as well; no doubt your competitors are striving to deliver superior attributes other than price. So to remain competitive or, even better, gain the status of industry leader or best in class, you and your organization must constantly provide

Teachable Points

your product or service at an extraordinary level, a level that truly excites the customer.

Let's pause here and review a customer satisfaction tool that would serve you and your organization quite well, especially if your competitors are not using it: the categorization and quantification of customer satisfaction. The method was developed by Dr. Noriaki Kano,[4] a Japanese engineer and consultant and quality expert, to analyze what customers expect in terms of quality and to measure their perception of a service provided. In the business quality environment, Dr. Kano's methodology is generally known as the Kano Analysis or the Kano Model Analysis.

Dr. Kano's model defines three levels of customer satisfaction. The model is not complicated, but it clearly reveals how customer satisfaction can make a quantitative difference in a competitive business environment. Here are Dr. Kano's three customer satisfaction levels:

- **"Dissatisfiers" (basic requirements):** This is the baseline of what your customer expects of your product or service. If you or your organization performs at this level, your customer will evaluate your efforts as simply ordinary—nothing unusual or deserving of special notice. This level of service does not excite your customers, and continually performing at this level will not improve their satisfaction or their perception of your product or service. However, they will become dissatisfied if your performance falls short of what they expect. In a nutshell, being judged as ordinary is no way to distinguish yourself or your organization from your competitors. More important, according to Dr. Kano, if you or your organization continually performs at that basic requirement level, there will be no improvement in your customers' perception of your performance or that of your organization.

- **"Satisfiers" (more is better):** The goal of any business operation is to deliver a product or service that exceeds the baseline level of service. Customers usually focus on certain requirements or specifications that improve the value of their product. Meeting those clearly identified requirements or specifications on a continuous basis can improve how the customer perceives your product or service. The more often you meet those specific requirements, the more your customer satisfaction rating will increase. Dr. Kano's analysis shows a direct correlation between meeting specific service characteristics and customer satisfaction.

- **"Delighters" (beyond expectations):** This level of service distinguishes an organization's product or service offerings from its competitors'. Your customers get great satisfaction when the level of service is extraordinary, going well beyond their expectations or even reaching an unanticipated level of service. What makes this category unique is that even if you're not actively delivering extraordinary service, the customer will not be dissatisfied; in fact, your customer satisfaction rating will not fall below a baseline satisfaction rating. In other words, your organization has achieved the reputation of offering excellent service.

The point of this brief overview is to emphasize that as a frontline supervisor, you must recognize that there are degrees of customer satisfaction and understand not just what your DCCs expect of you, but what excites them. You need to know the one or two things you can do for them that will "hit the ball out of the park," thus strengthening your organization's competitive advantage.

Remember, customer satisfaction is a critical strategic goal for any organization, so frontline supervisors must stay focused on that goal and not drift away from it. In any successful business, the focus stays on the customer, and as a result, the organization achieves its strategic financial goals. Now, we know that you, the frontline supervisor, are not in finance, but how you take care of the customer is what makes it possible for your organization to reach its financial goals. So, right where you are, you can influence the sustainability and profitability of your organization.

Profitability is a critical strategic goal for any organization, and it largely depends on customer satisfaction. In business, it's generally accepted that there is a direct correlation between financial stability and customer satisfaction. So while "It's the customer, stupid" is not a philosophy that requires deep thought, it's one that the frontline supervisor simply cannot afford to ignore.

Being On Point

As a frontline supervisor, you deal with customer requirements specific to your area and work processes. That's why you must develop and maintain a strong functional relationship with your Direct Customer Contact (DCC). You see, you are the point man—the one out front, the first to see it like the customer sees it and, when necessary, sound the alert and trigger a proper response. Being on point means you're in a pretty strategic position, and how you handle this responsibility helps determine whether your organization continues to be worthy of the customer's business. So it is critical that you find out what things are important to the customers right where you are. To keep your DCCs satisfied, you must remain focused: always listening and always ready to respond to shifting business circumstances.

Being on point really is a position of trust. You see, the frontline supervisor is in the position to protect his/her company's interests and continued success in accomplishing its primary purpose: to exceed the customer's requirements and product or service specifications while developing and implementing superior internal operating efficiencies. The military uses an acronym, SALUTE, to remind the point man of the fundamental information for which he is responsible: Size, Activity, Location, Unit, Transportation, and Equipment. When accurate SALUTE information is provided by the point man, the military planners will have what they need to structure and deploy the assets necessary to defeat the enemy, ideally with zero casualties.

In business, too, we use many generally accepted acronyms as shorthand for important business principles. In business, the term *zero casualties* translates to *zero defects*, and we can modify the acronym SALUTE to apply to that business principle. I would suggest that in order to achieve zero defects, we apply the following concepts: Search, Accurate, Logical, Unity, Tactical, and Effectiveness & Efficiency. Let's take a closer look at those concepts:

Search: The nature of business is to expect circumstances that will require problem resolution or adapting to changes in your organization's business environment. Such challenges shouldn't become bulkheads that allow problems to remain hidden and unresolved, literally permitting poor performance to prevail. It is important to remember that proper analysis will always reveal nonproductive events or problems. The key for frontline supervisors is to remain focused on their work and to notice, define, document, and resolve the root causes of a specific problem. They must be close enough to the work to clearly identify the root of any problems they encounter. That way they have the best chance to prevent a failure before it happens.

Accurate: Gathering data is essential to problem resolution, and it's critical that the data is correct and specific to the circumstances, because any decision made to mitigate problems must be based on what the data says.

Logical: When you identify a problem, your goal should be to develop an effective solution with a good plan to help you achieve it. Remember, though, that any plan developed and implemented must make sense. A plan that is effectively implemented must include appropriate control measures to ensure that any improvements achieved are sustainable.

Unity: Effective resolutions are usually cross-functional: analyzing a problem successfully typically requires input from internal sources that are beyond the boundaries of one person or one department. The simplest way to describe the concept of functional unity is "teamwork."

Tactical: How you go about solving a problem can determine the degree to which you succeed. The best methods for resolving or preventing the occurrence of problems or nonproductive events must be preemptive, efficient, and effective enough to prevent the unsuccessful or poor use of valuable productive resources.

Effectiveness & Efficiency: It is critical that you develop solutions that are targeted specifically to the problem and well-implemented. Doing the right (effective) thing well (efficiently) will usually yield positive results.

Transforming the military SALUTE methodology to management principles simply reinforces the generally accepted strategy of prevention versus detection. In the military, that strategy is critical; without its near-perfect execution, it has the potential of permitting the occurrence of serious human consequences. Here is an important fact: the magnitude of the prevention-versus-detection strategy is just as critical in the business world, too

Service Commitment

Your customers expect you to deliver the kind of service you and your organization have promised. And that's the customer's right; after all, your organization has essentially told your customers, "You can count on us," or "Relax, we've got your back." Here is how you, the frontline supervisor, fit into that promise: you are obligated to perform and deliver on that commitment, so you must make sure all the people in your working group know how important their work is to the customer. It's a big mistake to let the customer be invisible to your subordinates. There is a degree of difficulty, however, in keeping the customer front and center in the minds of all your subordinates and others in your group. That's because the customer can be unpredictable in requesting service transactions or responding to services delivered.

Sometimes customers can confuse matters by making requests that seem to be in conflict with what you are working to achieve in their best interest. They may fail to follow established methods and processes when they request a service or they will change their requirements, specifications, or expectations for service, and often with short notice. Your job as the frontline supervisor is to manage these shifting forces assignable to the customer in a manner that discourages your subordinates from judging the customer's performance as unsatisfactory. Because customers can be unpredictable, only a collective commitment—from you, your subordinates, and your peers—will turn the promise of service into reality and do so as a normal course of business. That means always delivering service that meets your customer's expectations, even when you're faced with changing

Teachable Points

circumstances and unexpected challenges initiated by the customer.

You may deal with hundreds of service events each day. Delivering an acceptable level of service is not a commercially engineered product. With an engineered product, every step is structured, heavily machine-dependent, and predictable. And a well-engineered product will likely warn you ahead of time that failure is coming your way so that you can take proactive measures to prevent it. In the service business, however, you usually do not have that kind of advance warning. Your work is certainly not mechanical, but rather your work is more about the people and the process, but still you must be on the right track and moving at the right speed with people in order to meet all service commitments as promised. In business, any routine or process developed and implemented has a life, and it can be a short one. That's because it's subject to frequent changes or alterations, made immediately or gradually, at the behest of the customer. Are changing customer demands unpredictable? Yes, but now you know that. And so I like to say that customers are "predictably unpredictable"—and that means you must develop and maintain functional knowledge about what to expect, and sometimes what not to expect, from your customers. The pathway to functional knowledge about your customers is to listen to what they say to you. Always monitor your DCC's feedback on how he or she perceives your work.

Predictably Unpredictable

Maintaining a smooth, predictable workflow can be very difficult, especially when satisfying an individual customer at the point of delivery—which is where you are. As a frontline supervisor, you'll have many customers to service, with shifting demands. You'll frequently be asked to provide the same service in different ways. Keep in mind that your customers have to meet the service requirements of *their* customers; like you, they are working in a competitive environment with shifting forces. Those shifting forces, caused by their customers' demands, may impact how you react to and meet their requirements. No doubt your customers will sometimes receive late notice from their customers, and when that or some other event causes them to make a change, it's likely that you will be affected or influenced by that event. Your customers certainly will not refuse the service order from their customer because they think you won't be able to perform; they'll take the order and expect nothing less than near-perfect performance from you. You can't predict when your customers will have these sorts of difficulties, but you do know that such things happen.

They're predictably unpredictable.
So your customers aren't predictably unpredictable because they choose to be. They face shifting forces, too, because their customers are also predictably unpredictable. When you can predict that the customer is unpredictable, you can sometimes plan for the occurrence of unpredictable events, and perhaps prevent a reactive response and execute a proactive response.

You are at the point of delivering the service as promised. Be prepared to meet special requirements, respond to unusual circumstances, and make special arrangements or customize when necessary. But take steps to ensure that the change will be feasible and practical. It's also important always to solicit the customer's input or reasons why the change is needed. You see, delivering quality service is a two-way process. Customer input is a critical factor if the service or product output is to meet acceptable quality standards. For example, you and your organization are better positioned to deliver excellent, reliable service if the customer provides excellent, reliable input: better marks, timely bookings for service events, proper documentation, and full use of system capabilities. It is critically important to work with your DCCs to get their input and requirements. Ask them specific questions: What has changed for you right now? How are you doing right now? Given the fact that change is constant at the point of delivery, asking such questions is a prerequisite to delivering an output that will be acceptable to your DCC.

One way to deal with a predictably unpredictable business environment, therefore, is to develop and maintain a rapport with your direct customer contact. It is imperative that you develop a partnership with your DCCs so that they know it's your goal to make sure they are taken care of. You want them to have a good experience when working with you; you want them to know that what they expect of you will happen. That reassurance will give you more flexibility in the day-to-day dynamics of business transactions. Personalizing your customer's experience can give him/her a view of your work from your perspective— and believe me, that is quite an accomplishment. In today's business environment, maintaining that kind of interpersonal relationship could yield a competitive advantage for you and your organization, so make that one of your highest priorities.

We've talked about the fact that customers see your shortfalls, because shortfalls cost them in terms of money, time, rework, and customer dissatisfaction. In a way, you have to see what your customers see; your view must be from their perspective, from their side of the equation. When you and your customer have a partnership that is clearly in your customer's interest, you increase the probability that your DCC will work with you collaboratively—keeping you posted on things and giving you advance notice about those things that are critical to him or her at the moment. In exchange, you must deliver the right service at the right time: that is the way to put credit in your personal account. When you eliminate shortfalls, the customer will see you as a service provider and not as a servant. That kind of relationship is something you must develop with your DCCs, right where you are. Once you do, you'll hear words like these from your DCCs:

- "Let me keep you posted."
- "Let me give you a heads-up on a developing event."

Make it your personal goal to hear these words, because they can give you an anticipatory advantage when the unexpected is just around the corner and not in plain view.

Service and Yesterday's Value

In many ways, providing service is like time. You cannot inventory time, and likewise, you can't inventory service. You can't stockpile it. Service is a forward-facing initiative. Once you deliver quality service, you must do it again. Your customers owe neither you nor your organization anything extra for delivering quality service. In fact, they expect good service; that's what they pay for. So they only "see" your service if it's below standards. Furthermore, the customer won't look back on your excellent service yesterday and excuse poor delivery of service or product failures today. The customer does not see today's service failure through the prism of yesterday's success. You see, a prism bends the light. Your customer will not bend the light if you fail to deliver service today as promised. Is that fair? To them it is, and that's all that matters.

After you've delivered an acceptable level of service, it recycles back to a value of zero. Your customer is focused on the service you deliver today, and so that must be your focus, too. Recycling back to a value of zero simply means you must repeatedly meet your customers' requirements. That is how you keep them from becoming dissatisfied. You must deliver quality service again and again and again and again and again . . . sorry. The bottom line is

Teachable Points

this: your customers do not expect failure from you, so if there is failure, that is all they'll see.

In business, you must continuously deliver exceptional service because the customer's demand for exceptional service is continuous. Therefore, what you and your staff present to the customer must be delivered in a near-perfect manner with every transaction. Yesterday's good performance only counted yesterday. It is likely that yesterday's performance carries little or no weight in the customer's evaluation of today's work. Today's work stands alone. Most customers don't conduct a weighted-average evaluation of an organization's services. If one of yours does, you're lucky, but it would be a rare occurrence and certainly not repeatable. Such an evaluation—what I call, a "weighted-average service evaluation" (WASE)—is something that you should not count on.

Concentric Circle
Organizational Structure
"The Customer": The Central Focal Point

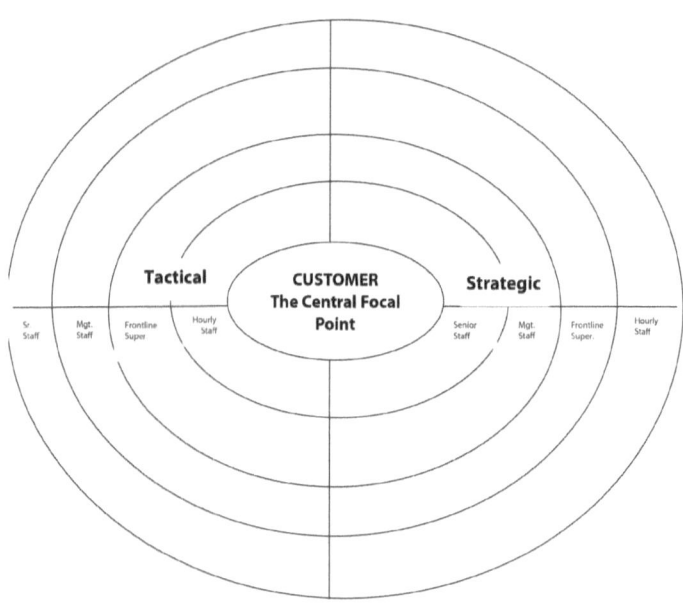

**The Concentric Circle Model
Developed by Reginald W. Sykes Sr.**

Concentric Circles

Concentric circles—a group of circles all having the same center—are a powerful graphic view of an organizational structure. In a business organization, the customer is the center circle—the customer is the central focal point. The customer is the reason any organization produces a product or service; it is clear, then, that the customer requires the organization's undivided attention. Everyone in the organization has some level of involvement with the customer; the concentric circles analogy shows how the customer is what I call "wrapped around" by everyone in the organization, whose intent is to offer a product or service that exceeds the customer's expectations. While customers are willing to pay for the service or product offered, their willingness to pay is conditional: what's offered at the right price must also meet their requirements and specifications. Meeting those specifications is what you must do to sustain a viable business relationship. Never forget that customers have the right to choose another vendor to provide them with the same product or service that your organization is providing. That is why it is critical that you listen to your DCC and discern exactly what the customer is asking of you.

It is important to understand that there are two sides to a business structure: a tactical side and a strategic side. Each concentric circle has a designated level of staffing on each side with defined responsibilities, and all the circles have a common goal. The hourly staff is in the circle closest to the customer, on the tactical side. On the strategic side of the circle are the senior staff, and they ask this question: "What are your infrastructural needs?" Their answer must be "Yes, we can meet those needs." On the tactical side, the question to the customer is "What are your Critical to Quality (CTQ) requirements?"—and again, the answer must be "Yes, we can meet those requirements." As illustrated by the concentric circles model, there is an internal, two-way feedback loop that facilitates what I call a "harmonized, planning-doing, customer-focused organization" (HPD-CFO). In its simplest form, the concentric circles model illustrates the integrated process of planning and doing.

One unique and positive aspect of the concentric circles model is that senior staff on the strategic side is informed, via the feedback loop, of day-to-day operations, but senior staff does not actively participate in the tactics of getting the job done. Senior staff's location on the tactical side, however, positions them to feed forward the value of the organization's strategic plan and some strategic insights on its execution. The concentric circles also give a pretty good outside-in customer perspective of an organization. With excellent service performance, customers can see the center circle, see themselves in the center, and see the positive results attained by the synchronized efforts of a horizontally structured organization working from the center out, with one goal: the customer.

The outside-in view also is likely to influence a frontline supervisor's DCC to quickly initiate outside-in QTC information that helps the supervisor stay responsive and on track to exceed standards. Giving the customer such a view—from the outside in—can help you earn a customer's loyalty because he or she can see that you and your organization are working in his/her best interest. Therefore, the outside-in view can also give you a competitive advantage, but you and your subordinates, along with those in each circle, must live up to the internal commitment of exceeding the customer's expectations. Doing more than what is expected to drive customer retention further establishes a competitive mind-set at every staffing level within your organization.

This type of structure really prevents a hidden view of the customer and his/her value to an organization. The concentric circles model offers a clear strategic view of the customer and enhances an organization's effort to deliver super service while running a super-efficient operation. I call that a "double-positive outcome"

Teachable Points

(DPO). Effectively coordinating tactical and strategic purposes is natural to business performance and an essential requirement for successful outcomes. The concentric circles model clearly illustrates this connection and effectively breaks the traditional, vertical business structure—that is, the kind with a bottom and a top. The vertical structure leaves the door open for a nonproductive attitude that can drive each staffing group to operate on a strictly functional level—you know, "I got mine, you get yours."

All business organizations are structured, but the structure we are discussing here is horizontal, not vertical. A horizontal organizational structure makes a positive difference in the service industry, as it gives everyone a view of the customer from the same perspective: the customer's. You see, your perspective, or that of others in your organization, tends to be filtered by internal biases that blur your view and don't align with the customer's view. Taking care of the external customer becomes very difficult when internal biases are allowed to prevail.

A significant benefit of the horizontal view is that it positions senior staff, via the feedback loop, to ensure that everyone understands the concept of positive customer impact and the value of the customer to the organization. In a horizontally structured business, everyone shares the same goal, including the hourly staff, because their view is on the same level as that of senior staff. The hourly staff actually has the ability to touch the customer and therefore can impact the customer, just as the senior staff can. Therefore, it is critical that the hourly staffers—those who are closest to the product or service—are routinely included in informative internal customer-focused communications. Customer-focused performance is the driving force to developing and maintaining a viable business relationship with all customers, so it is vitally important that employees at every level within the organization have the same operational perspective of the term *customer service*. The concentric circles model allows a proactive view of the customer that positions an organization to deliver competitive customer service, and that makes 100 percent customer satisfaction an obtainable goal.

The key to this model is that each circle feeds the circle in front of it, handing off pertinent and timely process information, functional tools, and critical customer-focused information. This system keeps service commitments on track while also motivating customers to acknowledge excellent performance. It also highlights the important business principle of the *internal customer*. You see, the circle in front of you is really your immediate customer. Whatever individual or group work that is done at the job level, on the floor, in the shop, or in the office will be handed off to another individual or group who will continue that process until the final output is presented to the external customer. During that transformation of input resources, the value of the relationships between internal customers and across job functions cannot be overstated. There must be communication among everyone involved in the process with input responsibilities. Your organization can achieve a competitive level of customer satisfaction only if its internal customer processes are the focus of everyone in the organization.

With the concentric circles organizational model, the important point to understand is this: all participants in a business process must be just as committed to their internal customer as to their external customer. Each circle, by design, is complementary to the circle it feeds. This is a fundamental business principle, and if not baked into the attitude of everyone in the organization, then the internal resources allocated to a product or service will result in an unsatisfied external customer. Satisfying the external customer is the primary purpose of all employees involved in a business process, and it should mandate a commitment from all of them to see and treat each other like customers. How well you satisfy your internal customers determines the quality of the product or service delivered to the external customer.

Teachable Points

Remember, the quality of an organization's product or services reflects how well its internal customers integrate their individual contributions to the business process.

Each staffing group, including your subordinates, has the most experience with and functional knowledge about what's happening within their own circle, so each group must mutually agree to provide actionable information about the process to those in the next circle with functional responsibility for the next operational or transactional step. When all players in a process share information in this way, competing organizations will likely find it difficult to match their performance. Whether the information comes from the tactical side or the strategic side of the circle, it all leads to the same place: the customer. Look again at how close the hourly staff is to the customer in the horizontal model. But those staff members have to be aware of that proximity and how their efforts can produce positive customer results. This is a critical factor in an organization's success and therefore worthy of constant review. If your hourly subordinates do not know how close they are and how their work can influence the customer's evaluation of the organization's performance, then you have lost the opportunity to deliver service that exceeds the customer's expectations. It is therefore very important to "talk customer" with your subordinates on a routine basis.

Let's use another sports metaphor: say, a relay race. Imagine your subordinates with the "service" baton in their hands; they represent you and your organization at the point of handoff—the point where the baton *must not* be dropped. That is how important your subordinates are. So it is the frontline supervisor's responsibility to ensure that the service or product is in near-perfect order when handed off. Your customers expect a good handoff from you and your organization—it's not necessarily a noticeable event when the baton is handed off properly. But if the baton is dropped, your customers will take notice quickly, because then neither you nor your customer can finish the race. By the time you cross the finish line, the race will be over: the customer will have experienced the negative effects of a poor handoff.

The best way to ensure a good handoff is to effectively handle the day-to-day process variances that can prevent an excellent outcome. These variances may be caused by internal or external circumstances, so the frontline supervisor must be extremely cognizant of them. Through process analysis, the frontline supervisor must determine the reason(s) for any variation, act quickly to minimize them, and make sure that significant or unusual variations do not negatively impact a successful outcome—a good handoff. Remember, there will always be variations in a business process, and so there will always be the need to make adjustments, but only when a variation is assignable to special causes. And any adjustment must also add value to the customer. Don't take corrective actions or make process adjustments based only on your personal perspective. Such tunnel vision could negatively impact other internal business processes and must be avoided as a matter of course. While there will always be some variations in any process, the goal is to minimize them, keeping them as close as possible (plus or minus) to what you've determined to be normal, or shall we say the center.

Remember that efficiencies must not stop at your department's door or your organization's door; they must push open and reach into your customer's door, especially that of your DCC. When you allow your DCCs to see and feel that you and your staff have a high level of interest in their priorities, you can positively influence customers' evaluation of your organization and strengthen their interest in you, the frontline supervisor. The primary reason for good internal business processes, excellent personal performance, and proper execution of the baton handoff is simply to keep the customer satisfied.

5

Your Performance: Back to Basics

a. The three Cs
   i. Communication
   ii. Cooperation
   iii. Commitment

b. Learn to Dialogue
c. Good, Better, Better, Better ...
d. Nine Points to Master

Communication

We all can agree that communication is essential to conducting business. In fact, a viable business relationship cannot be effective absent effective communication among those involved in the business process, both internal and external. Effective communication with the customer is of course critical, but internal, customer-focused communication with your peers, subordinates, and superiors is just as important. That's not news—in fact, it's likely that everyone in your organization understands the importance of communicating. So why, then, do some business organizations still have communication problems, and what are their primary causes? One typical cause is clearly identifiable and often assignable to most individuals in an organization, and that is the tendency to evaluate the intended message from their perspective only. When they do that, they're not really listening to the message.

In business communications, you want to get a good sense of the *other* person's point of view. The goal is to clearly understand the intended message—and that starts with you, the listener. Dr. Peter Drucker,[5] one of the great management gurus of our times, validates that the listener, the person designated to receive a message, is the communicator, and that understanding that dynamic is the gateway to effective communication. The Bible tells us to "be quick to listen, slow to speak"—and I would add that there is nothing wrong with a little "divine intervention" if that's what it takes to improve your listening skills. It is not a complicated business principle, but it's an important one: if the person intended to receive a message does not hear or understand it, then effective communication has not happened.

When you are communicating (listening), you are sharing knowledge and learning, too. You see, the purpose of the intended message is to enhance your understanding of a topic or to share information that would allow you to take appropriate action on an important issue. So in order to learn and maintain good communication skills, you must practice listening. Look for opportunities to improve your group or one-on-one listening skills, and always work on being interested in what others are saying to you. Communicating effectively—really listening—is something you must continually practice. Learning is a never-ending process, and there's always something new to learn, so don't take communication off your learning list. When you pay attention to your own communication skills, especially when your failure to communicate effectively causes a problem, you are more likely to correct those errors going forward.

If you are the speaker, convey your knowledge, your subject-matter expertise. You want others to *want* to listen to you, and you must be persuasive, because your goal is for the listener to accept your intended message. So clearly express your intentions or concerns, and then ascertain that the listener has communicated by how he or she responds. Ask yourself a few questions. Did the listener get the message? Did you hear the listener's feedback? Did you become the listener? If the listener's feedback was not appropriate, did you convey your message again but with more clarity and precision? Did the listener get the message the second time around? By asking these questions you know where you stand, which is the first step to improving your communication skills.

We all come from different backgrounds—different cultures, circumstances, or schools—and that makes each of us different. It is critically important, however, not to allow personal differences to inhibit your ability to communicate. Remember, we still have plenty in common, too—enough to know the negative impact of not listening. Practicing what you know to be correct makes good sense. So why not just listen?

Learn to Dialogue

One of the major components of teamwork is dialogue. Imagine a discussion of an important business topic when no one is engaged in listening. There is no debating the fact that not listening can lead to failure in business processes and is harmful to any business environment. By not listening, you negate any opportunity to have a meaningful conversation—real communication. It is okay to suspend your own assumptions in order to listen. When you do so, you're not surrendering your perspective; you're just setting it aside. You're allowing the message to come through unfiltered, because once it's filtered, the intent of a clearly defined and appropriately delivered message is lost. You must hear the other person's perspective, or effective communication cannot happen.

Cooperation

Remember, you are part of a team that shares a common mission to enhance departmental and organizational business performance, so always be helpful. Certainly, team members can disagree or have differences in opinions, and that's not necessarily a bad thing. Conflict can spark conversation, which has the potential to enhance a team's performance. Conversation connects the speaker and the listener, pushing team members beyond the blockage of disagreements and facilitating mutual and operational understanding of the team's goals and how to reach them.

You cannot do your job well or function as an effective team member if you go solo; business processes and organizations simply are not structured that way. Your job and what your team is working to achieve are part of a business process, and your role is just a piece of that process. That piece was handed off to you, and you'll hand it off to the person or group in charge of the next operational or transactional step in the process. Remember this: a business process only passes through your function, so when you pass it back out, make sure it's in good order, as expected. The key to a successful process is employees' willingness to collaborate with each other and share information, which grows the knowledge base within your working group, your department, and your organization. Sharing information adds value to your efforts, which in turn adds value to your team. It is especially valuable to a team's mission to share your knowledge about the customer, your situational instincts, and your tricks of the trade—you know, the stuff you've discovered that really, really works. That is the true value of teamwork: the exponential growth of functional knowledge in a structured business environment.

Whether a business process passes through your purview successfully depends upon your performance. You can keep a positive outcome on track or you can take it off-track—it's your choice. Your performance determines that. You see, *cooperation* is a commonly used word in discussions of teamwork. But *collaboration* is the real key to cooperation. Collaboration takes cooperation to the highest level—to use the vernacular, it's cooperation on steroids. When individuals are collaborating, each one understands and is reaching for a common goal. By each of you doing your individual share—what I call your "tailored share"—and by working collaboratively, you will reach that common goal, and all at the same time. When you are collaborating, your efforts are mutual and supportive, compounding your ability to achieve your organizational goals and objectives.

Collaboration is a collective effort: every partner in the process must be aware of everyone else's activities. An effective team structure usually involves interdepartmental team members working as a unit toward meeting a common goal. A good adjective to describe this structure is *complementary*—the team members are partners, managing in harmony. Frontline supervisors must understand that their function may differ from that of other partners, but their assignments, though different and often independent, are part of the same business process. Managing in harmony is the best way to keep a process on track and moving at the right speed—that is, at the customer's pace. You see, if you are to reach the desired outcome, you must accept that doing so depends on your personal performance as well as that of the others in your group: your participating partners or team members.

Commitment

It is essential that you commit yourself fully to your job. Just putting in the time and going through the motions will not get the job done. Success belongs to those who are committed, and it takes highly committed people to continuously improve their processes and quality of service. And that's critical to customer satisfaction. Why? Well, because customers are demanding more each day. They want continuous improvements in service, and they want the service or product delivered to add value to their operation. In business, commitment to the mission must be collective. That sense of commitment, reflected in an organization's culture, is quite necessary for achieving sustainable, customer-focused success. Collective commitment means everyone involved in every active business process is totally committed to contributing to the company's success. If you have collective commitment within your organization, that's one of the best ways to ensure that your company's performance consistently exceeds your customers' expectations. As a frontline supervisor, your job is to make sure that your subordinates follow your lead in valuing commitment—that they are just as committed as you are in meeting goals and exceeding expectations.

It takes a team effort to effectively address a business project. That's because business processes cross departmental boundaries, as many departments are involved in any business process. No one process begins and ends at one desk, with one person, or in one department. As I stated earlier, a business process only passes through your functional area—it doesn't stay there; it's passed on to the next operational step. In business, cross-functional processes should not be an exception. This is a fact; however, usually it is not acknowledged or practiced in many organizations, to their great detriment. Often organizations see themselves as a collection of departments. That really is an outdated view. Business functions are simply parts of a process, and it is a fundamental business rule that a process is finished only when the service or product is delivered to the customer as promised and in conformance with the customer's requirements. Delivering a service or product as promised requires everyone at every level in an organization to fully commit to performing his or her assignments collaboratively—that is, working in harmony as expected.

Good, Better, Better, Better...

Regardless of your best efforts, there is always more you can do to improve. You can always do more to make your work product better, but you must be consistent in your efforts to do so. The concept is "Good, better, better, better . . ." rather than "Good, better, best." That must be the prevailing attitude of the frontline supervisor, and an attitude that must be tapped into. You must never let there be an end to your goal of improving—put a period behind that. You see, once you believe that you have achieved your very best, then what? You stop the business principle of continuous improvement, that's what. And why is doing better always the goal? Because your customers are usually in a competitive environment, and in order to be competitive in their business environment, they too must deliver as promised. Customer service and financial results are factored into your customers' strategic planning—and how you and your organization perform can influence what your customers deliver to their customers. The outcome of your business processes can impact your customers' strategic financial plans. That's how important you are to your customers. What you do affects their profit margin. A reduction in profit margin caused by your organization's performance is an outcome that no customer will tolerate. That is why doing better, both internally and externally, must always be an agenda item for you, the frontline supervisor. Never doubt what you can achieve by always working to improve.

Dr. Martin Luther King once said, "If you don't have sustained, disciplined action, you don't have an organization." While Dr. King was one of the great men of our time, he was not generally recognized for his management skills (although they were obvious from the magnitude of his accomplishments) as much as for his tremendous leadership and persuasive skills. However, his words here are nothing less than a management principle. Think about the phrase *sustained, disciplined action*: there is no better way to describe what is required of a frontline supervisor, who must always be looking for ways to do good work even better.

Nine Points to Master:

1. Communication

Effective communication with customers, peers, subordinates, and supervisors is essential to good business. Remember, however, that truly effective communication must be targeted to the listener. Communication does not happen if the intended message is not received, so you must work on delivering (speaking) your message in a manner that connects with your listener. You must also learn to become the listener even as you're delivering your message. Feedback is important; it influences how you deliver your message. So learn to navigate the waters between being the speaker and becoming the listener. If your listening skills are weak, you cannot effectively communicate your intended message, and you probably will not make happen what you intended to make happen, and consequently you will fail to meet expectations.

2. Focus versus Tunnel Vision

Maintaining a steady focus is necessary if you want to complete your duties successfully. But that doesn't mean you should have tunnel vision—not paying attention to who or what impacts you, or who or what you are impacting, but just doing your thing. Well, guess what? It is not just "your thing." Your function is to input designated resources into specific business processes, knowing that there are others in your group or in other departments inputting their resources into the same business process. It is only through the collaborative efforts of all suppliers of input that the product or service delivered—the output—will exceed the quality standard promised by the organization. This is a fundamental business principle, and tunnel vision just doesn't fit with it. Certainly this narrow view inhibits any opportunity to meet internal or external customer-focused commitments. So tunnel vision is, as they say, not an option.

3. Part of a System

You must think and act knowing that you are part of a system. Learn to use the system, but work within it. You must accomplish your personal and departmental tasks so that individuals, groups, or departments can accomplish theirs. The system is what connects all functions within an organization and can determine its overall effectiveness. Your objectives, as well as those of your department and the company as a whole, are better achieved if you work in concert with the system. If you avoid the system in order to make your own job easier, you will cause the system to be less effective and less efficient, and you will certainly have a negative impact on your organization. You must not allow how you go about doing your job to become a constraint to the system. The negative impact caused by your actions may not be evident to you for a while, but at some point the system will reveal the results of your actions, and the organization will feel the magnitude of any negative impact of your decision to work outside the system.

4. Working with the Internal Customer

In a business environment, the frontline supervisor must know the answer to several very important questions. They aren't complicated, but not knowing or not following up on the answers will generate at best an unsatisfactory process performance. Such an outcome would, of course, be discomfiting to your internal customers, those within your group to whom you are providing resources so that they can do their jobs. Here are the questions all frontline supervisors should ask themselves: *What do other individuals, groups, or departments need from me? When do they need it?* And more important, *What is the negative impact if I fail to deliver the critical "whats"?* Knowing the correct answer to each question and doing the things necessary for a good outcome will have a positive impact not only on your personal performance but also on the overall performance of your organization. If at any point you can't give a thorough and acceptable response to any of these questions, you must initiate whatever appropriate action is necessary to do so.

Remember, your function contributes to all the business processes you are engaged in. Therefore, don't focus solely on the priorities directly assignable to you, because it's not just you—or, as I put it earlier, it's not just "your thing." You are responsible for providing input into many processes, so provide them on time and in good order—that is, correctly. You see, if what you hand off to the next step—your subordinates, your peers, or senior staff—is incomplete or incorrect, then internal efficiency stops dead in its tracks. Work has to be redone (rework), the process time increases, costs increase, and if the problem isn't corrected in time, a defective product or service will be handed off to your internal customer or, worse, your external customer—an outcome that can cost you even more than the dollars you'll spend on "reworking" or fixing the problem.

There is a process improvement tool used in the Six Sigma methodology that diagrams the business process by categorizing its major components into five integrative, progressive steps: Supplier, Input, Process, Output, and Customer (SIPOC).[6] Although the intent here is not to fully drill down into the SIPOC tool, the first two steps, Supplier and Input, can help

Teachable Points

further explain the idea of passing the baton "in good order." You see, as a frontline supervisor functioning as an active participant in a business process and in the context of the SIPOC process tool, you and your subordinates are Suppliers, and you also hand off the Input resources to team members (internal customers) with next-step responsibilities, enabling them to successfully complete their task.

You see, any supplier to a process has the responsibility of ensuring that his/her input—including time, information, materials, and other resources—is no less than what the individual, group, or department is expecting, given that they intend to use or apply that input without having to manipulate it. The point is this: the resources input by suppliers are interrelated components of a business process, and it is that internal process that transforms their input into output—the products or services that are ultimately delivered to the external customer. That is why all suppliers must understand the magnitude of their responsibility and actively practice the *internal customer concept*, ensuring that their input into the process is accurate and timely. It is these two components of the business process—Supplier and Input—that must be given proper attention in order to facilitate a seamless handoff to the next step in a business process. To be a truly effective frontline supervisor, you must actively practice the internal customer concept described in this book and accept responsibility for the fact that your input affects others' ability to meet and exceed customer expectations.

You also must understand the value of interrelationships. You can achieve better results when you have no boundaries in your interactions with others. Jack Welch, the renowned former CEO of General Electric, coined the term *boundarylessness*.[7] So, what does *boundarylessness* mean, anyway? From my perspective, it means allowing others in your group to tap into your thoughts, knowledge, and skills to expand their capabilities and their contribution to organizational commitments. Of course, there is also a reciprocal component inherent to the concept of *boundarylessness*: it removes any barriers between staff, peers, supervisors, subordinates, departments, and of course the customer. Within this context, your individual objectives are part of your department's objectives. Your performance must complement your department's performance, which extends into your company's performance. Success in your function or your company's mission simply cannot be achieved where functional independence prevails. Therefore, effective frontline supervisors must be aware of their interactive skills and gauge their own effectiveness when collaborating with their subordinates and others in their group. Removing boundaries is clearly an effective way to maximize the value of working with others.

5. Preventing Problems

You should aim to eliminate the cause(s) of problems and shortcomings before they occur. This is the functional definition of prevention, and it must be the constant focus of the frontline supervisor. Routinely detecting and resolving errors or shortcomings after they occur is ineffective and costly. A famous author that I cannot identify once said, "An ounce of prevention is worth a pound of intervention." As I mentioned earlier, firefighting prevents conditions that cause a fire. It's not simply fire-damage control, which prevents further damage but doesn't eliminate the damage or prevent reoccurrence of the same failure. An effective way to prevent problems is to continually analyze your work processes and operating systems. Always think about what you and your subordinates are working to accomplish. Give constant thought to how the work is done—not in order to affix blame, but to find and fix circumstances that would allow the occurrence of a problem. Then put control measures in place that will keep the potential problem from resurfacing. The purpose of controlling an improved business

Teachable Points

process is to maintain any gains achieved after implementing an improvement plan. Holding on to those gains by preventing defects or shortfalls equals continuous savings. Preventing errors certainly benefits the customer, but it also generates internal cost savings that improve your organization's ability to achieve its financial objectives.

One way to guarantee that you will have a problem is to give less thought to your work and assume that you have no problems (and we all know what happens when the word *assume* is divided into three segments . . .). If you're assuming, you are not thinking about your task as you work through it. Instead you should be asking yourself some questions: *What's the impact of my work on the customer? Am I meeting my departmental and personal goals?* You can answer yes to these questions only if you are constantly thinking about the work you do.

Facilitating a good work process and working well with your operating system is, in fact, being *proactive*—doing well what you should be doing well anyway. Measuring the outcome of your work is a key factor in detecting problems and errors. If you are not measuring on a continuous basis, how do you know whether improvement is or is not needed? When measuring correctly, you can recognize and move to improve performance problems and eliminate or mitigate any identifiable constraints before anyone else sees them and before you experience an unfavorable outcome. If you don't measure your performance, you'll find yourself working on problems from behind the curve—and that means your customers, internal and external, will feel the effects of unresolved problems. Working behind the curve also means that the impact or magnitude of the problem will grow, usually resulting in additional cost and, worse, complaints from the external customer. That is not a good outcome; in fact, it is poor performance, and poor performance equals a poor outcome.

Here are a few more points on measuring:

First of all, it is a long-standing principle that it is best to use facts and data to measure your current performance. Before you can initiate any improvements to a process, you must use data to determine its current status. It is critical that you establish your baseline performance. It has been said, "You can't get to where you want to go if you don't know where you are starting from."

You evaluate the baseline facts and data and form a response plan based on that evaluation. You see, if you don't measure your inputs and outputs, you might not be aware of a problem or its impact, and you won't know how your current performance measures up against internal and external expectations. You also may not know who is being affected by a problem you're unaware of; so while the problem may remain hidden, the cost of the problem is real. Making assumptions or using gut feelings to evaluate and adjust the work process is useful only if you are working to resolve very insignificant problems.

If you are not measuring your performance, the ultimate result will likely be an unsatisfactory outcome for your customer, and any related problem with your performance will probably remain unresolved, becoming a recurring event that necessitates rework, waste, and, more important, customer dissatisfaction. (And remember, customer satisfaction is your primary objective.) Keep in mind: you are not measuring the results of your work just to reproduce the past, although measuring can give you a clear view of the past, which is important and necessary. You are measuring, however, to chart a clear path for the future. You need data to tell you whether you are headed in the right direction and whether you are meeting your internal and external objectives—and if you're not, measuring can drive corrective action and initiatives designed to get you back on track. In other words, you must be able to positively influence the outcome of what you are measuring. Otherwise, why bother measuring at all?

6. Continuous Process Review

It is expected that you will aim for continuous process improvement; a continuous review of your work assignments will always reveal improvement opportunities. There are always practical ways of doing even more with less. You can identify them by using process improvement tools such as Six Sigma, a management methodology that focuses on eliminating defects in a service or product by meeting Critical to Quality requirements set by the customer and by promoting internal operating efficiencies.[8] Another methodology to explore is the Theory of Constraint (TOC), a system designed to reduce process lead time by eliminating or minimizing any constraints in a process that add no value to it or that prevent it from achieving its target performance level.[9] By the way, you'll always find such a constraint in any business process if you are looking diligently to improve it.

Some business-process-improvement initiatives, like Six Sigma and TOC, require top-down commitment. But sometimes it is difficult to get senior staff on board with significant changes, so kicking off new ideas may have to start with you. It's wise to begin by doing a little research on some proven management tools. Then you can do some studying and a little research and perhaps make a strong presentation to senior staff. Even if your idea is not accepted, you've learned something new that could enhance your own professional capability and personal performance as well as those of your subordinates (I'm just saying . . .). Your job as a frontline supervisor is to continually seek out new ways to strengthen weaknesses or eliminate defects and constraints—to always strive to make things better. That includes your personal growth.

The dynamics of your day-to-day responsibilities can impact your procedures and processes, so make sure you continuously review them. By doing so you can reduce or eliminate rework caused by errors due to poor procedures or processes that create opportunities for poor execution. Your goal should always be to improve how the work is performed—and it is usually your *process,* not your staff, that allows errors or defects to happen. Keep in mind, rework is not just the cost of doing business; it is a decrease in productivity and therefore a business loss. Rework uses assets, but it doesn't add value to the company, to the customer, or to you—the point man. Look at it this way: a recurring event that requires repetitive use of resources but produces little or no gain is simply a bad proposition. The Japanese call such an occurrence *muda,* but in the English language, the word is *waste.*

There is another good reason why continuous process improvement must be a basic and permanent goal for a frontline supervisor: in business, you can expect shifts in any process over time, because the goalpost is constantly shifting. Why? There are two critically important reasons. First, your customers' needs are always changing, and second, your competitors are constantly seeking new advantages. If you aren't making continuous improvements, your competitors likely will find advantages—or you will have given them advantages. You see, the need to improve is a constant factor in conducting business. So if you are not continuously improving, you've stopped contributing to your organization's commitment to exceptional service. There is no better way to squander your organization's competitive edge.

Remember that most industries are highly competitive, and your customers are usually deep in competition. That is what drives the dynamics of your side of the business ledger. Your customers' needs and changing requirements are driven by the competitive nature of your industry and theirs. The input from your customers must change as *their* customers change their input to them. In today's competitive business environment, change is now a natural function of process execution, so if you just keep doing what you've been doing, all you will get is what you already have. You have heard a thousand variations on this theme, because it is a proven fact. There is no need to prove it again. If you don't change when necessary, you don't progress; in fact, you retrograde and advance to the rear—and the competitive status of your organization is diminished.

7. Applying Logic to Work

Labor usually is a pretty hefty percentage of the cost of doing business. Still, it is wise to view labor cost as an investment, and your focus should be on the return on that investment (ROI). So it is important to make sure that good logic is applied to every task that is performed in your areas of responsibility. "Good logic" means weeding out bad work practices and bottlenecks, because constraints in workflow equal an increase in process time, which leads to an increase in labor cost. Even when you have deployed good logic in your work, you still must not be satisfied with where you are, because things change. In a changing environment, the question is how do you cope with change? First, you must understand the reason for the change; second, you must understand the magnitude of the change; and third, you must adapt or be flexible in response to change. The goal is to remain stable in a changing environment.

But even with logic applied in the workplace, your people still play a significant role in production gains. Among your subordinates there is plenty of experience and knowledge, and it's essential that you use it. That's best done by expanding your subordinates' knowledge about the customers and the business processes that they are a part of. Your employees also have teachable moments. Those moments come from their day-to-day experience on the job, where they see logical opportunities to improve how they do their work. They can use their experience to develop teachable points that they can share with you, but you must let them do that. I can recall many times when I have observed others sharing their teachable points— like when George Clark shared his knowledge of break-bulk heavy lifting, when Trish Hagan taught team members how to skillfully navigate in and around the Navis Gate Operating System, and when Mae Jo Gordy shared her insights into handling CBP's administrative work. You must routinely link your people's knowledge to accomplishing your daily task—it's just the smart thing to do. How do you do that? You communicate with them, you collaborate with them, and, more important, you let them make a contribution to the work, especially when their input generates significant improvement opportunities. The more your subordinates know that their contribution matters to the customer, the more they will strive to increase the value of their contribution.

8. Inspecting versus Expecting

The renowned Dr. W. Edwards Deming, who enumerated the Fourteen Obligations of Top Management, advises managers to "cease dependence upon inspection as a way to achieve quality." His point is that your work process should be good enough to produce a quality product without an inspection step as part of the process. My impression from Dr. Deming's language and from my own observation is that, unfortunately, inspection is still an active step in business processes even to this day. So let's take a closer look at the subject.

Inspection means taking measures (steps) at various points in a production or transactional process to ensure that specifications are within the tolerance level as established by the customer. Inspection adds preventive cost to a business process and may to a degree increase lead time, but it also provides additional assurance that the end product will meet the customer's Critical to Quality (CTQ) requirements the first time around. Of course, it

Teachable Points

costs less to inspect than it does to fix an error after the product or service reaches the customer, but the cost of inspection should never be dismissed as insignificant. In spite of the cost, though, it is clear that inspection adds value to any process. Therefore, any resources used in the inspection have value, too.

Inspection is the process or step that makes near-perfect quality not just possible, but achievable over time. That's why it is important to push for near-perfection in all your tasks or functions, all the time. By inspecting, you'll get closer and closer to that mark. In fact, inspection can be considered an investment. Beyond ensuring that your process meets specifications, inspection may include a continuous review of processes and procedures, double-checking the current status of the work, and ensuring in advance that resources and tools are available.

As a frontline supervisor, don't just show up on the floor in response to problems or complaints. You should show up (inspect) when things are going well, and let your subordinates know that all is going well. It is a good practice for a frontline supervisor to regularly see the work firsthand. Certainly you can understand the workflow better if you are out there, so there is nothing wrong with frequent visits. Always document why the work is going well, build what you learn from your walk-around into your processes, and then lock in the lessons learned. By doing so, you'll minimize the "find it and fix it" method of maintaining a steady process for your staff.

If you are inspecting like this regularly, I assure you that you will continually improve your process and production gains and that you will more consistently achieve your desired results. You can virtually eliminate service failures and the cost of failure if you follow this simple rule: It is not what you expect, it is what you inspect.

While both *expecting* and *inspecting* are about outcome, there is a big difference between expecting an outcome and inspecting so that you can achieve an outcome as expected. *Expecting* is simply waiting for a task or process to be completed and then evaluating the quality of the outcome. *Inspecting* is being in direct contact with the task or the process while it's happening. In-process inspection is like steering your car as you drive to keep it in the center of your lane. It may include taking corrective action before the product or service is delivered to the customer. Here are some examples of in-process inspection/steering:

- Ensuring that proper resources are available, in place, and on time is a preventive action.
- Offering advice and problem resolution while a task or process is happening is a "Teachable Points" action.
- Tracking a task or process to ensure that completion will be on time with an outcome that meets the customer's requirements is a customer service action.
- Inspecting as a means of providing assistance and guidance to your subordinates is a management-training or educational action.

Make sure your subordinates know what you are inspecting. You are evaluating the functioning of the process and procedures. Are they working? Are there inherent problems with them? What is the impact of the outcome? By inspecting, you'll get the answers to these questions. Inspection is important because of the frequency of operating changes, internal and external. Customer requirements and exceptions and your internal processes all have the capacity to shift—and they will. That is a fact.

Here is a little golden nugget for you: a good business process should be so tight that there's no need to inspect. And so in theory, I agree with Dr. W. Edwards Deming. The goal of management should be to eliminate the need to inspect as a method of producing a quality product or service, and to eliminate reactive responses that find and fix shortfalls after a product or service is presented to the internal or external customer. Dr. Deming's operating methodology is to keep improving the system to a standard that does not allow errors to occur.

But I also feel that until all aspects of a process are near-perfect, you must inspect.

9. Production Gains in the Context of Change

Change is now a function of the work process, so it's more important than ever to keep tabs on the status of the work: Where are we? Are we headed in the right direction? Are we taking appropriate steps to complete our assignments on time and in good order? If you don't see a problem today, you certainly will tomorrow. You see, production gains cannot happen in a passive environment, where problems aren't resolved and so their negative impact is realized.

Sufficient production gains do not happen even in a *reactive* environment—you know, where you work aggressively to solve a problem only after it has come to your attention. That's like fire-damage control. You might have put the fire out, but you've also felt its effect and assessed its cost. It is better to prevent fires by having a proactive environment. Being proactive is a manifestation of your intellectual drive. That is why you must always keep your intellectual drive high, because it will be manifested in near-perfect personal performance. Intellectual drive means doing things differently and always doing them better. You have to stay mentally sharp because if you aren't, you can't be proactive. Steady production gains cannot happen unless you are continually thinking of ways to maintain a proactive work environment that involves employees at every level. You can include them in the "high intellectual drive" initiative by valuing their intellect.

6

Managing Your Personnel

a) Getting Results through People
b) Trust and Reputation

Getting results through people is a goal that a frontline supervisor must pursue with vigor. Your subordinates are your most valuable asset and active resource; they do the work, and they have an abundance of good ideas. There is always enough knowledge and know-how in the ranks to get things done better—but only if you involve your people in the process and give them opportunities to achieve. Look for and create opportunities for your subordinates to show their stuff by delegating challenging work assignments so that they can put their good ideas to use. Believe it or not, their ideas for process methods could be better than the methods you're currently implementing, so if you fail to tap into those ideas, you'll be squandering a powerful resource. You'll have missed a chance to increase productivity, which is not a cost-cutting initiative but rather a cost-savings initiative.

Productivity gains must always be on your agenda, and effectively communicating with your subordinates about their work is essential to productivity. It is a smart move to let your subordinates show you how they can execute their assignments. *Execution* is a powerful business term meaning carrying out the plan exactly as prescribed. In this case, the term reflects how your subordinates are actually doing their work. Getting results

Teachable Points

through people is a critical path to successfully executing any plan. Often your subordinates, based on what they've learned on the job and through their observations of outcomes, have made adjustments to make their own work more productive—and in doing so they have measurably increased the productivity of the process as a whole. So it is smart to have regular conversations with your subordinates about any positive adjustments they've made on their own in performing their job and to encourage them to continue looking for ways to improve. Your subordinates can make a difference in the quality of the work, but they have to know that—so tell them.

You see, to be a truly effective frontline supervisor, you must have a double commitment: you must be committed to both your people and the work. Your subordinates can provide timely feedback on your procedures and processes, positioning you to evaluate the quality of the work from your subordinates' perspective and make appropriate adjustments when necessary. (Remember to assign credit for any positive results to your subordinates' input.) No doubt there will be times when your subordinates encounter problems on the job that they would defer to you to handle. Make sure they understand that when problems are reported, your focus will be on correcting the process and the cause of the problem, not assigning blame to the workers. You must also make it clear that reporting problems encountered in the workplace is not considered negative feedback. Labeling it that way might keep them from reporting essential performance information. Keeping the work process "squared away" and problem-free is your responsibility as the frontline supervisor, and so you must encourage your subordinates to keep you posted if and when problems occur. It is simply the smart thing to do.

Your subordinates' feedback really is a means of teaching and learning, so tell them what you've learned from them. Then let your subordinates see what they are teaching you and how their timely feedback is helping to ensure that the product or service delivered to your DCC meets all quality standards, which makes the service delivered to the customer effective and efficient for your organization. Keep in mind that when your subordinates are on the job and performing the work well, there is a triple benefit: your customers are okay, your company is okay, and your subordinates are okay. They need to know that they are an integral part of that achievement—and that absent their input, a positive, customer-focused outcome is less likely.

It's safe to say that most of your subordinates want to do a good job. But can they do it working for you, and will you *let* them do it? These are fair and often necessary questions, and you, the frontline supervisor, control the answers. Find those subordinates who have leadership skills and welcome their ideas about improving the task they are charged with performing. Allowing their input into how the work is done promotes a "stakeholder" attitude among your subordinates. There is nothing wrong with having a lead person out in the field or on the floor. Being a lead man or lead woman certainly is a gateway to intrinsic motivation.

When you present leadership opportunities to subordinates, you inspire enthusiasm—and that's what you want in your workforce. Remember, intrinsic motivation has its own engine; the motivation comes from within the person. Your job as a frontline supervisor is to give your workers a reason to turn on their engine, and that means you have to be influential. Giving your subordinates an avenue to see the results of their work is one way of doing this; it will encourage them to follow your lead and will keep them interested in the company's well-being, which translates to increased productivity. Remember, subordinates working in their own interest will extend themselves to working in the interest of the company.

Teachable Points

It is important to develop and maintain strong relationships with your subordinates, establishing a work environment that increases productivity. Communicating—in other words, listening and, more important, letting your subordinates *know* you are listening—also means that you learn from them, teach them, and collaborate with them. And again, make it a point to acknowledge your subordinates' contributions. Figure out the best way to do so, whether privately or in an open forum, depending on the individual.

It would be wonderful if all employees were self-motivated and did not require a push from you. But for some employees, that's just not the reality. Fortunately, you have influence that can make it a reality for those who need growth in this critical area. So it's your job to construct and maintain a work environment that fosters motivation. If you don't do it, who will?

I think we can agree that motivation is a complex human trait. We also can agree that while a frontline supervisor is not a psychologist, he or she can have some impact on subordinates' motivation. The key is to recognize their achievements—that's a powerful motivation tool. Be creative in doing this, but save recognition for those who have earned it—those who have gone beyond what is expected, stepping outside their assigned area to make a special contribution for their coworkers and superiors.

Remember, an employee who goes above and beyond what is required is good for your organization, too—not a bad return for targeted investment in personnel. That kind of special performance earns recognition, so make sure that you give it when it's earned. By doing so, you strengthen your subordinates' willingness to continue exceeding expectations. They will always want to do better—and that attitude functionally defines the term *intrinsic motivation*. A subordinate who is enthusiastic about the work is a good measure of an effective work environment.

Your effectiveness as a motivator depends to a large degree on your ability to lead and direct. Facilitate, don't control; simplify, don't complicate. Keep in mind that your subordinates are aware of their own talents, so give all of them the opportunity to contribute to the fullest extent of their capabilities—let them release their energy on the job. Work to inspire them; when they are inspired, they will see how to and desire to perform their duties even better. *Inspire, and then get out of the way!*

Keep in mind that everyone has a potential performance level; usually you can't go any higher or do any better than your potential. The same principle applies to your subordinates. Right now, your performance and that of your subordinates probably is less than your potential. Your performance level today is simply what you and your subordinates are capable of achieving right now. You can raise that level, but only if you work at it diligently. Again, your push to achieve more should never be finished. It is important to understand this essential fact: the gap between your potential performance and your actual performance can be defined as "waste." That's right, performance not achieved is waste. Your job as a frontline supervisor is to narrow that gap for yourself, your subordinates, and your organization. Lead the way by making the work more productive. An efficient process and orderly work procedures will contribute to your employees' ability to achieve their potential. Remember, it is through achievement that your employees will be satisfied. Achievement can be self-fulfilling, and by facilitating their ability to achieve, you are fostering self-generating enthusiasm. I've seen it myself: enthusiasm is transferable. As a frontline supervisor, you can have a positive impact on your subordinates, and they can have a positive impact on you.

As a lead person, you must keep your message simple, consistent, and constant. That will keep you connected with your employees. You must also develop and implement effective work procedures and processes, because how you design and lay out work assignments is what will keep your subordinates on track and making steady progress in reaching their potential. Establishing logical work assignments is the best way to prevent poor performance by your subordinates. Remember that routine work processes and instructions should not require extraordinary performance just to do a "normal" day's work; when you're trying to resolve a problem, the first place to look is at your work process, not your people. That puts the ball squarely in your court. If you really want to solve the problem of excess lead time or other nonproductive events, it is always best to identify what part of the process is causing bottlenecks and delays.

Your job is to keep customers satisfied by knowing and exceeding their requirements, and effective personnel management is critical to that role. Remember how close your subordinates are to the customer—look again at the concentric circles model. Remind your people of where they are in that structure and the difference they could make. Given how close they are to the customer, it is reasonable to incorporate their knowledge and insight into any process-improvement initiative you undertake. Your subordinates are involved in the day-to-day dynamics of the work, so you must facilitate an informative feedback loop with them that can positively influence operational efficiencies. In fact, this is a great way to inspect the work while it's still in process and without additional cost. So the feedback loop is something you must cultivate and encourage. Often your subordinates will have improvement ideas just sitting there, uncultivated—but you have to reach out and tap into them. You see, what your subordinates usually focus on is fixing problems they have deemed ineffective, a waste of their own time and energy, so they'll adapt a process to better fit their way of doing the work. An effective frontline supervisor will keep his/her subordinates informed of and focused on the positive influence they can have on the work and the customer. The more aware employees are of their influence, the more they will strive to make their impact continuous and even more significant.

Here is a little something you can wrap your mind around: it is generally the frontline supervisor's *subordinates* who can suggest the improvement ideas that are the most timely, practical, and productive. That is why their feedback is so important and must not be dismissed. This discussion opened with the premise that your knowledge must not remain tacit; well, the same is true of your subordinates' knowledge. So give them an avenue for making their knowledge explicit: talk with them, ask for their input, implement any reasonable ideas they offer, and of course give them credit for their contribution.

Your subordinates can offer you reliable ways to make things better. After all, who knows the ins and outs of their job, and what they can potentially contribute, as well as they do? Inviting their suggestions for improvement serves two purposes. First, it will inspire them to continually seek improvement opportunities when doing their job. Second, it will encourage them to follow your lead, given that you've consistently welcomed and shown appreciation for their advice. Here is a little golden nugget for you: your subordinates' willingness to offer improvement ideas will help you routinely exceed departmental expectations. You see, their willingness really matters. When you collaborate with your subordinates, you keep the door to customer-focused improvement "locked in the open position," as I like to say. Don't close the door on what I call "subordinate-based opportunities" (SBOs) to make customer-focused improvements generated by the tactical staff in the circle closest to the customer. Your subordinates contribute to the quality standards you are working to achieve, so SBOs should always be on your radar screen. When you get a ping, tap into that improvement opportunity, and you'll find your people right there, ready and willing to make the work processes they are engaged in even better.

It is interesting that as we conclude this discussion, we've returned to the topic of the customer, because the customer is not just the endpoint of your or your organization's efforts—the customer is the endpoint and the starting point, too. The economic well-being of any organization depends on its effectiveness and efficiency in all matters concerning the customer. Effective personnel management related to customer service is quite necessary to achieving specific goals for customer satisfaction. Your subordinates must understand the impact that their performance can have on the customer, and they should know how their performance factors into the customer's evaluation of your organization. Again, consider the concentric circles organizational structure: the customer might be in the center, but who is right next to the customer on the tactical side? As clearly indicated, it is your subordinates. So it is important that you take extra care to ensure that each subordinate knows how his/her function adds value to the outcome promised to the customer.

Trust and Reputation

All the discussion points and supervisory principles presented up until now are valuable and worthy of pursuit, but they also are conditional. In order to effectively practice the teaching points and generally accepted management principles described here, the frontline supervisor must operate from a base of honesty, because trust is the foundation of motivation. If your subordinates do not think you are sincere and trustworthy, you will not achieve the results that can be achieved through them. On the contrary, you will end up with very poor results, and that will be a direct reflection on your personal performance. Building and maintaining trust is a critically important factor in managing your staff. Losing trust would be a major setback for a frontline supervisor. And trust begins with your good reputation.

You know, it takes awhile and a lot of good work to build a good reputation, but once you've done so, you've paved the path to earning the trust and respect of your subordinates. In the workplace, you have to prove yourself before you can earn trust—and your good reputation is what proves that you're trustworthy.

And just as it takes awhile to earn trust, it takes a long time to regain it. So as a good frontline supervisor, it is your responsibility not to lose this vital business asset, the trust of your subordinates.

Notes

1. George Eckes, *The Six Sigma Revolution* (New York: John Wiley & Sons, 2001, page 51).

2. Villanova University, *Comprehensive Six Sigma Green Belt Handbook* (2007).

3. Jens J. Dahlgaard, Kai Kristensen, and Gopaal K. Kanji, *Fundamentals of Total Quality Management* (Denmark: Nelson Thornes Press, 2002).

4. Villanova University, V-14.

5. Peter F. Drucker, *Management* (New York: Harper & Row, 1973).

6. Ashley Osgood, *The 2012 Handbook for New Quality Managers* (IBS America, 2012).

7. Robert Heller, *Jack Welch* (New York: Dorling Kindersley Book, 2001).

8. Peter S. Pande, Robert P. Neuman, and Roland R. Cavanagh, *The Six Sigma Way* (New York: McGraw Hill, 2000).

9. Donald W. Benbow and T. M. Kubiak, *The Certified Six Sigma Black Belt Handbook* (Milwaukee: American Society for Quality, Quality Press, 2005).

www.ingramcontent.com/pod-product-compliance
Lightning Source LLC
Chambersburg PA
CBHW030902180526
45163CB00004B/1677